8

Mémère's Country Creole Cookbook

The Southern Table
Cynthia LeJeune Nobles, Series Editor

MÉMÈRE'S

COUNTRY CREOLE
COOKBOOK

Recipes and
Memories
from
Louisiana's
German
Coast

NANCY TREGRE WILSON

LOUISIANA STATE UNIVERSITY PRESS BATON ROUGE

Published by Louisiana State University Press
Copyright © 2018 by Louisiana State University Press
All rights reserved
Manufactured in the United States of America
FIRST PRINTING

Designer: Michelle A. Neustrom
Typeface: Livory
Printer and binder: Sheridan Books, Inc.

Mam Papaul's™ is a trademark used by permission.

Family photos are from the author's collection.

Library of Congress Cataloging-in-Publication Data

Names: Wilson, Nancy Tregre, 1942– author.
Title: Memere's country Creole cookbook : recipes and memories from
    Louisiana's German coast / Nancy Tregre Wilson.
Description: Baton Rouge : Louisiana State University Press, [2018] | Series:
    The Southern table | Includes bibliographical references and index.
Identifiers: LCCN 2017038122| ISBN 978-0-8071-6897-4 (cloth : alk. paper) |
    ISBN 978-0-8071-6898-1 (pdf) | ISBN 978-0-8071-6899-8 (epub)
Subjects: LCSH: Cooking, Creole. | Cooking, Cajun. | Cooking,
    American—Louisiana style. | LCGFT: Cookbooks.
Classification: LCC TX715.2.L68 W555 2018 | DDC 641.59763—dc23
LC record available at https://lccn.loc.gov/2017038122

This book is dedicated to my children: Angela, Tregg, Charlena, and Nanette.
I hope that I have answered questions about our family
that they have not yet thought to ask.

CONTENTS

Acknowledgments

I WANT TO EXPRESS MY GRATITUDE to my husband, who has given me constant support for this project. He has eaten everything that I have cooked from flan to tripe, driven me everywhere I have felt I needed to go, and accepted my strange sleeping habits without complaint.

It has been fun cooking with my long-time friends Mary Ann and Jara, two foodies who are just as crazy about cooking as I am. They helped me figure out how my mom cooked goose, piglet, and turtle. I am grateful for their input.

My older relatives Una and Joe answered questions that I had not thought to ask my mama Lelia or my grandmothers Mam Papaul and Mémère when they were still living. And I am grateful to two "cousins-in-law": Nunnie, who provided genealogical information about Mémère Nellie; and Jeanne, who supplied details on nine generations of Faucheuxs, Kellers, Zeringues, and Schexnayders.

Thanks to Brenda Madere, who shared a very special picture of the bread delivery wagon that my mom talked about. The photo and details Brenda offered brought my mom's story to life.

Thanks to my cousin Morris, who has kept the boucherie tradition alive in the family. And I was so excited that my young friend Bert found his parents' backyard bridal party photo because I was one of the flower girls. He also provided family recipes for sausage and hogshead cheese.

I am also grateful to the River Region Arts and Humanities Council for a grant to help cover the cost of photography.

What would I have done without my very competent editors Cynthia Nobles, James Long, Catherine Kadair, and Susan Murray. They have done nothing but make the book better with their meticulous attention to detail.

Mémère's Country Creole Cookbook

Mam Papaul and her mother, Mémère

INTRODUCTION

THIS COOKBOOK TELLS THE STORY of the unique "Country Creole" foods created by the early settlers of the Côte des Allemands, Louisiana's German Coast. This place that I call home is about twenty miles upriver from New Orleans. It's made up of St. Charles and St. John the Baptist Parishes and is bisected by the Mississippi River. My large family has been here for almost two hundred years. My French-speaking German relatives arrived from the Alsace-Lorraine area of Europe in 1721; French ancestors arrived in the 1780s. My three daughters and my son were determined not to marry anyone from Hahnville, the parish seat of St. Charles Parish and our hometown, for fear they would wed a relative. Had they married anyone from what we call the River Parishes, which include St. James Parish to the north, that would prob-ably have been the case.

The Mémère named in the title of this book was my French and German great-grandmother, Nellie (pronounced Na'lee) Schexnayder Zeringue. She grew up in St. John the Baptist Parish. Mémère learned early on how to cook the native produce, game, fish, and fowl found in the area, and she learned how to make French pastries and desserts from her mother. After her husband died, she and her two daughters, Octavie (nicknamed "Tavie") and Chloe, lived with her parents and later with her sister Tante 'Deel (Odelia Haydel) and her family. Octavie grew up helping her mother cook for the families who befriended them after her father's death. When Octavie married Leo-pold Faucheux, who was of European French descent, she became known as "Mam Papaul." Up until the 1960s, many families on Louisiana's German Coast still spoke French. In the local French dialect, "Mam" means "Madame." My grandfather's nickname was "Papaul." Together they had nine children, but they always had place for anyone in the family who was in need. After Octavie married, Mémère lived with her and her husband until she died at age eighty-nine.

Under Mémère's tutelage, Mam Papaul became a genius in the kitchen, teaching her daughters how to keep their families healthy and happy with good food. In turn, Mam Papaul taught my mother, Lelia, and her four sisters to become expert cooks and bakers. My mother developed a cottage industry baking birthday and wedding cakes. This heritage survives today. I became a home economics teacher and the owner of a food manufacturing business. I developed a line of specialty Creole dinner mixes, velvet cake and frosting mixes, New Orleans–style dessert mixes, and a Mardi Gras king cake. My eldest daughter is a graduate of the Culinary Institute of America and is a pastry chef.

Mam Papaul was also the brand name I chose for the line of products that my family manufactured. My husband, Charles, and I started the business with my mom and dad, Lelia (Faucheux) and Urbin Tregre. After my parents passed away, Charles and I bought out the corporate shares my siblings inherited, and we became the company's sole owners. We were the first in the world to make Cajun and Creole boxed dinner mixes. Those early products included gumbo, jambalaya, étouffée, corn soup, and dirty rice. In all, I have successfully developed sixteen recipes for the Mam Papaul line. I am often asked why the line of specialty food products that I developed is called Mam Papaul's. It is because of this heritage.

Why do I use "Creole" rather than "Cajun" in this book's title? "Creole" best describes the people of the German Coast. "Creole" is a seventeenth-century word from the Spanish *criollo*, which designates a person of European descent born in some part of the world other than Europe. We on the German Coast are mainly descendants of early Germans, Canadian French, European French, and Spanish. When the first Germans arrived here in 1721, the European French centered in nearby New Orleans were the dominating force in government and were, therefore, most influential in the daily affairs of the German Coast. By the time the Acadians arrived, the Germans had been here more than forty years and had already developed their own traditional ways of cooking with local ingredients. German Coast cuisine resulted from collaborations among all the ethnic groups who settled here. It would be almost impossible to determine which elements to attribute to each group. Many generations created our brand of cuisine, each facing the challenge of adapting what they knew to what was available and sharing their cooking discoveries with their friends and families. The Cajun French influence on everything was fairly strong, with many non-French in the area, such as Mam Papaul, growing up believing they were French. Cajun French was spoken in my relatives' homes, even into the 1960s, and we served many Cajun French dishes, but our cooking was decidedly Creole. Even though the German Coast started out German, the French influence dominated our region, especially in

My mother, Lelia Faucheux

the areas of food, language, and religion, which, to this day, is predominantly Roman Catholic.

My grandmother Mam Papaul was born in 1894 in Convent, Louisiana. In 1920, she and my grandfather moved to Hahnville, where they bought a Queen Anne–style, wood-frame cottage that I now own and have lived in for most of my fifty years of marriage. I still remember Mam Papaul on the screened back porch as she washed dishes in a large pan filled with heated water from the cistern. Eventually, she had a nice kitchen with a gas range, but for many years she cooked on a wood-burning stove in a room built off that screened porch.

Like most residents of the German Coast, Mam Papaul was a devout Catholic; she helped keep the church clean, organized church fairs, and was always available to help with other church-related activities. Since she was a fantastic cook, she was often called on to help prepare lunch when the archbishop visited our parish. She was also good friends with the rectory housekeeper, who was the priest's sister. That family was from Germany, and through them, Mam Papaul learned to enjoy unfamiliar foods, such as Limburger cheese, crabapples, and artichokes.

I obviously inherited Mam Papaul's love of cooking. Since I was six years old, I've been stirring together flour and oil to make roux, a crucial thickener in south Louisiana cooking. That knowledge proved beneficial when I started my business, when we were the only ones who made authentic dried roux for a gumbo mix. There certainly were copycats, but the competition used caramel color to make their dried gumbo brown. My company made dried roux by going through the dangerous process of browning flour in pizza ovens. Eventually, I found a manufacturer that did this tricky work for us.

Over time, Mam Papaul's line of foods came to include New Orleans–style mixes for scampi, okra gumbo, sauce piquante, crawfish pie, pralines, bananas Foster, and bread pudding, as well as red bean and gourmet seasoning mixes. In addition, we made the first line of cake mixes manufactured in Louisiana, and we offered flavors such as Mardi Gras King Cake, Red Velvet Cake, Black Velvet Cake, and Lemon Velvet Cake.

I sold my line of food products several years ago. Now I spend much of my time documenting the stories of my family and the history and food of the German Coast. I hope you will enjoy reading some of these stories as you delve into the cuisine of my south Louisiana ancestors.

Cooking in the kitchen with my youngest daughter, Nanette.
This was Mam Papaul's kitchen when I was growing up.

Soups and Gumbos

IN MAM PAPAUL'S HOUSE, as in the homes of the rest of my family, a salad would never suffice for a meal, but our hearty soups sure would. Growing up on the German Coast, we enjoyed a variety of soups, even during the summer. What went in those soups depended on what was growing in the backyard garden. A favorite summer soup was crab and okra gumbo, made with okra my dad grew. From June through August, we liked corn and shrimp soup made with fresh summer corn. Back when I was a child, which was during World War II and a time of shortages, our shrimp for this dish usually came from the Mississippi River. River shrimp were sweet and tiny; a large one might be no longer than a thumbnail.

Soups were important to early German Coast settlers, as were stews, which cooks thickened with relatively large amounts of dark roux. Roux is typically associated with the French, but Germans in the southwestern state of Swabia in Germany, as well as on Louisiana's German Coast, traditionally cook with a roux the color of a tarnished penny.

Many Cajuns live in my hometown of Hahnville, a town with a German name. I didn't realize I was German or that I lived on what was originally called the German Coast until I was in high school. While I was doing volunteer work for my neighbor, the school librarian, I found a raggedy copy of John Hanno Deiler's book on the German Coast of Louisiana. I asked if I should throw it away. "Why no," said the librarian, "that book tells of your German heritage." German? I thought everyone in the area was French! The adults in my family all spoke French and English, except Mémère, my maternal great-grandmother, Nellie Zeringue, who knew English but refused to speak it with her grandchildren. The café au lait, étouffée, gumbo, and *pain perdu* we all consumed on a regular basis were French. What was our librarian talking about? Even though neighbors had German surnames such as Schexnayder, Zeringue, Hymel, and Haydel, no one I knew in the area thought of themselves as German.

Corn and Shrimp Soup

Makes 6–8 servings

This was a summer favorite at my house, and we had it often. We just called this dish "corn soup" and expected it to be made with river shrimp. Imagine my surprise when I went to college in Lafayette, the large Cajun city in the southwest part of the state, and friends there told me they made corn soup with smoked sausage and potatoes. Right after I graduated from college, I lived in New Roads, a small town north of Baton Rouge, and a friend there made her corn soup with diced pork.

The seasoning in most of our food is simple, as it is in this soup: the Cajun "trinity" of onion, bell pepper, and celery, along with salt and pepper. Growing up, we didn't cook with herbs such as sage, basil, tarragon, or even rosemary. I have since learned that these herbs grow well in our area. For this recipe, if you don't have shrimp, you can substitute 1 pound of canned or fresh crabmeat, diced ham, frozen crawfish tails, or kielbasa sausage. You can even copy my Lafayette friend and use smoked sausage and potatoes. Mama finished many of her dishes with a little fresh green onion and a handful of chopped parsley, both of which are staples in German Coast gardens.

4 tablespoons vegetable oil
2 tablespoons all-purpose flour
¾ cup finely chopped celery
½ cup chopped bell pepper
½ cup finely chopped onion
4 cups shrimp stock, chicken stock, or water
1 (17-ounce) can creamed or whole-kernel corn with liquid
4 ounces tomato sauce
4 (4-inch) cobs of corn, boiled and cut into 1-inch pieces
1 pound shrimp, peeled and deveined
1 teaspoon salt
½ teaspoon black pepper
Hot buttered French bread for serving

1. Heat oil over medium heat in a heavy-bottomed, 5-quart soup pot. Add flour and cook, stirring constantly, to make a very light brown roux. Add celery, bell pepper, and onion. Cook, stirring constantly, until onion is translucent, about 10 minutes.
2. Add stock, canned corn, and tomato sauce. Bring to a boil and lower heat to a simmer. Cook 10 minutes. Add corn still on the cob and cook 10 more minutes.
3. Add shrimp, bring to a boil, and cook 8 minutes. Season with salt and pepper. Serve with hot buttered French bread.

White Crab and Shrimp Bisque

Makes 6–8 servings

Dark seafood bisques made with roux are common on the German Coast. If you say "white bisque" to a guest, the response could be negative—that is, until they get a taste of white seafood bisque.

1 pound claw or lump crabmeat, picked over for bits of shell
½ pound shrimp, peeled and deveined
2½ cups unseasoned seafood stock or water
1 tablespoon dry or powdered salt-based crab boil (found in local grocery stores or online)
½ cup (1 stick) unsalted butter
½ cup all-purpose flour
1½ cups (4 ounces) fresh mushrooms, sliced

1 cup finely chopped onion
6 tablespoons chopped green onions
2 tablespoons chopped green bell pepper
2 tablespoons finely chopped celery
3 cups half-and-half
2 large egg yolks
¾ cup sherry (optional)
2 tablespoons chopped parsley
¼ teaspoon freshly grated nutmeg
Salt and ground black pepper to taste

1. Place crabmeat and shrimp in a 3-quart saucepan. Add stock and crab boil. Bring to a boil, then reduce heat to a simmer. Cook until shrimp turn pink, about 4–5 minutes. Drain crab and shrimp, reserving both the seafood and the stock.
2. Melt butter in a 5-quart stockpot set over medium heat. Stir in flour and cook 2 minutes, stirring constantly. Add mushrooms, onion, green onions, bell pepper, and celery. Cook 10 minutes, stirring constantly.
3. Stir in reserved stock and cook 5 minutes. Add half-and-half and bring to a boil. Lower heat and simmer 10 minutes. Thin with additional stock, if desired.
4. Lightly beat egg yolks with a fork and whisk into soup. Add sherry and simmer 10 minutes.
5. Stir in reserved crabmeat and shrimp, parsley, and nutmeg. Check for seasoning and add salt and pepper, if needed. Serve hot in individual soup bowls.

When I was growing up, bisque took at least two days to make.
On the first day, we caught crawfish in the swamp.

Quick Brown Roux-Based Crawfish Bisque

Makes 8–10 servings

My whole family went crawfishing together, including Mémère Nellie all decked out in her very stiffly starched and ironed sunbonnet. After everyone ate their fill of boiled crawfish at my grandparents' house, we all pitched in to peel leftovers for the next day's bisque. Since making bisque is extremely time-consuming, I take a few shortcuts. When I have a few hours, I do stuff crawfish heads, but it's much easier to make balls out of crawfish filling, and they're just as tasty.

Filling for stuffing heads or making crawfish balls

½ cup (1 stick) unsalted butter
1¾ cups finely chopped celery
1¾ cups finely chopped onion
¾ cup finely chopped bell pepper
6 cloves garlic, finely minced
2 pounds Louisiana crawfish tails, fresh or frozen, rinsed in cold water and finely chopped
2 cups plain or seasoned bread crumbs

¾ cup water
¼ cup finely chopped parsley
1½ teaspoons salt
¼ teaspoon cayenne pepper
2 drops liquid crab boil (purchase at specialty stores)
24 cleaned crawfish heads (if stuffing heads)
4 egg whites

1. Melt butter in a large skillet and sauté celery, onion, bell pepper, and garlic until onion is translucent. Add crawfish, bread crumbs, water, parsley, salt, cayenne pepper, and crab boil. Mix well.
2. Preheat oven to 350°F. Stuff filling into crawfish heads, or use a tablespoon or small scoop to make 24 small balls. Reserve any remaining filling.
3. Beat egg whites until light and fluffy but not dry. Roll stuffed heads or balls in egg whites and bake on a well-oiled pan until browned, about 20 minutes. Set aside until ready to make bisque.

Bisque

2 packages Mam Papaul's Gumbo with Roux Mix (found at southern grocery or specialty stores or online)

3 quarts water, or a combination crawfish stock and water or chicken broth

24 stuffed crawfish heads or crawfish balls (see recipe above)

4 ounces tomato sauce

½ cup (1 stick) unsalted butter

½ teaspoon powdered bay leaf or 1 whole bay leaf

½ teaspoon dried thyme, or 1 teaspoon fresh

Salt and ground black pepper to taste

Hot cooked rice for serving

1. Place gumbo mix, water, baked crawfish heads or balls, and any extra stuffing in a 5-quart pot. Bring to a boil.
2. Add tomato sauce, butter, bay leaf, and thyme. Reduce heat and simmer 30 minutes or to desired thickness. Remove bay leaf, if whole. Add salt and pepper to taste. Serve hot over cooked rice.

Mémère is seated at the right in her ironed and starched sunbonnet.

Artichoke and Oyster Bisque
à la Corinne Dunbar

Makes 4–6 servings

This recipe is based on memories of lunch with my mother, aunts, and sisters at Corinne Dunbar's, a famous New Orleans restaurant once located on St. Charles Avenue. The restaurant has long since closed, but we enjoy this soup at home using my original recipe. We all agree this is a close duplicate.

1 large artichoke
1 lemon, cut in half, divided
½ teaspoon salt
4 tablespoons olive oil
4 tablespoons all-purpose flour
¾ cup chopped onion
½ cup finely chopped celery
4 cloves garlic, finely chopped
2 tablespoons minced fresh parsley
½ teaspoon dried thyme

½ teaspoon dried oregano
¼ teaspoon dried basil
1 bay leaf
2 chicken or seafood bouillon cubes,
	dissolved in 3½ cups hot water
½ pint or more oysters, chopped,
	reserving liquid
2 (14-ounce) cans artichoke hearts,
	chopped, liquid reserved
Buttered French bread for serving

1. Bring a large pot of water to boil. Add artichoke, ½ lemon, and salt. Cover the pot and boil briskly until the base of the artichoke is tender, about 40–45 minutes. Drain, reserving liquid. When artichoke is cool enough to handle, remove leaves and set them aside. Remove fuzzy choke and coarsely chop artichoke heart. Set aside.
2. Make a roux by heating olive oil in a 5-quart soup pot set over medium heat. Add flour and cook, stirring constantly, until roux is the color of peanut butter. Add onion, celery, and garlic. Cook, stirring constantly, until onions are translucent, about 5 minutes.
3. Add parsley, thyme, oregano, basil, bay leaf, dissolved bouillon, oyster liquid, juice of remaining ½ lemon, chopped artichoke hearts, and canned artichoke liquid. Simmer 20–25 minutes. If necessary, thin with reserved artichoke boiling liquid.
4. Add oysters and simmer 8 minutes. Remove bay leaf. Serve hot in individual bowls and garnish with reserved artichoke leaves. Don't forget the hot buttered French bread on the side.

Quick and Easy Gumbo Vert

Makes 6 servings

Gumbo vert is one of the dishes most closely associated with south Louisiana's Germans, who were, and still are, known for their agricultural prowess. Some people insist that gumbo vert, also known as green gumbo or gumbo z'herbes, should have seven greens, and many called it a soup. The following recipe makes a side dish, not a soup. As documented by Cynthia LeJeune Nobles in the edited volume *New Orleans Cuisine: Fourteen Signature Dishes and Their Histories,* this was a meatless dish the Germans in Louisiana cooked on Holy Thursday during Holy Week. Mama always cooked hers with spinach and mustard greens, the way most people in our area liked it. We did not eat beet, carrot, or turnip tops. We only ate the roots of those vegetables; tops were fed to the chickens or pigs. We also did not use cabbage or lettuce in this soup, as did many others, and we were unfamiliar with collards and kale. Of course, you can use as many greens as you like. Omit the meat if you want to stick to the way this dish was originally intended, as a meatless side dish served over white rice on Good Friday. If you want to turn this recipe into a soup, simply thin it with strong stock.

2 bunches fresh spinach, washed several times, or 2 (8-ounce) boxes frozen
2 cups water
2 bunches fresh mustard greens, washed several times, or 2 (8-ounce) boxes frozen
3 tablespoons vegetable oil
3 tablespoons all-purpose flour

4–6 ounces salt meat, rinsed and diced (optional)
¾ cup finely chopped onion
1 teaspoon finely chopped garlic
Pinch of sugar
Salt
Ground black pepper
Louisiana-style hot sauce
Hot cooked rice and buttered French bread for serving

1. Steam spinach and mustard greens in water until very tender. Drain and reserve liquid. Chop greens and set aside.
2. In a large, heavy-bottomed saucepan, make a roux by heating oil on medium heat. Add flour and cook, stirring constantly, until roux is golden brown. Add salt meat, onion, and garlic. Continue cooking 10 minutes.
3. Add greens, liquid from greens, and sugar. Simmer 30 minutes on low heat, stirring frequently. Season to taste with salt, pepper, and hot sauce. Serve hot over rice with a side of buttered French bread.

Andouille and Chicken Gumbo

Makes 12–16 servings

This is the gumbo my mother, Lelia (pronounced Lel-yah), made for the family to eat after Christmas Eve midnight mass. We also enjoyed it on Sundays and holidays. Compared to gumbo made in other areas of Louisiana, German Coast gumbo is generally thin. We start our recipes with roux, that thickener of browned oil and flour. Mom always made her gumbo with a hen, which gave the stock a hearty chicken flavor. Her andouille was a deeply smoked pork sausage made in the neighboring town of LaPlace, the self-proclaimed "Andouille Capital of the World."

There are only three things common to a chicken and andouille gumbo on the German Coast: chicken, smoked sausage, and a roux the color of a dark copper penny. During the cool-weather oyster season, many cooks add oysters. To stretch that pot of already economical gumbo, my grandmother would drop in raw eggs and cook them until they were firm. Lately, I have been copying my friend Mary Ann, who adds smoked turkey necks to fortify the flavor. My sister Joel adds chopped bell pepper, and my cousin Chokee likes to throw in mushrooms. Filé, ground leaves of the sassafras tree, can also be added for earthy flavor and thickening. Lucky is the person who has access to fresh homemade filé. Just remember to never sprinkle filé into a boiling pot of gumbo. That will make the gumbo slimy.

Mom, like everyone else I knew, never served gumbo without a side of potato salad (recipe page 104). Although this recipe serves a crowd, it can easily be downsized, and gumbo freezes well.

1 (4-pound) chicken or hen	1 pound smoked turkey, any parts
4 teaspoons salt	1 pound smoked andouille, or other
1 teaspoon ground black pepper	smoked pork sausage
5½ cups water, divided	½ cup chopped parsley
1 cup vegetable oil	⅓ cup chopped green onions,
1 cup all-purpose flour	green part only
2 cups chopped onion	Hot cooked rice for serving
2 cups chopped celery	Filé powder (optional)
½ cup chopped bell pepper	

1. Preheat oven to 350°F. Season chicken with salt and pepper and place in a large skillet or rimmed metal baking pan. Bake until browned, about 40 minutes. Remove chicken and set aside. Deglaze pan with ½ cup water and set aside.

2. Place remaining 5 cups water into a large pot or Dutch oven and bring to a boil.
3. Meanwhile, make roux. Heat oil in a large, heavy-bottomed saucepan over medium heat. Add flour and stir constantly until roux turns the color of a dark copper penny. Add onions, celery, and bell pepper. Cook until onions are translucent.
4. Add roux with seasonings, chicken, turkey, and andouille to the boiling water. Bring back to a boil, lower heat, and simmer until meats are tender, about 1½ hours.
5. Stir in parsley and green onions. Simmer five minutes. Remove chicken, andouille, and turkey. When cool enough to handle, remove the bones and skin from chicken and discard. Cut into serving-sized pieces. Cut andouille into serving-sized pieces and debone the turkey pieces. Place meats back into pot. Add additional salt and pepper, if desired. Serve gumbo hot over rice. If desired, season each plate of gumbo with filé.

Lelia with chicken

Okra Gumbo with Chicken

Makes 6–8 servings

Tastes in cooking often varied on the German Coast, even in close families. My mom always cooked okra gumbo with seafood, and that is still my favorite. But my aunt Aurelie liked okra gumbo cooked with chicken, as did my aunt Hedwidge, who made an excellent version of okra and chicken gumbo on her wood-burning stove at Pépère Tregre's house.

¼ cup, plus 3 tablespoons vegetable oil
1 pound fresh or frozen okra, sliced, or 1 (16-ounce) can, drained*
¼ cup all-purpose flour
1 medium tomato, peeled, seeded, and chopped
¾ cup chopped onion
⅓ cup chopped celery

2 tablespoons chopped bell pepper
2 cloves garlic, mashed
2 quarts chicken broth or water
6–8 pieces cooked chicken (store-bought roasted chicken is fine)
1 teaspoon salt
Pepper to taste
Hot cooked rice for serving

1. Preheat oven to 350°F. If using fresh or uncooked frozen okra, heat ¼ cup oil in a skillet and add okra. Sauté over medium-high heat until okra is no longer ropey, about 15 minutes.
2. Make a roux by heating remaining 3 tablespoons oil over medium heat in a Dutch oven. Add flour and cook, stirring constantly, until roux is the color of peanut butter. Add tomato, onion, celery, bell pepper, and garlic. Cook 10 minutes over medium heat, stirring constantly.
3. Add okra, broth, cooked chicken, salt, and pepper. Simmer 30 minutes. Serve hot in individual bowls over rice.

*With an abundance of okra from the garden each summer, many cooks roast and freeze it for later use. See Roasted Okra recipe, page 122.

Poule D'eaux Gumbo
(pronounced pool-doo)
Makes 6 servings

A *poule d'eaux*, also known as a marsh duck, is a small, short-beaked duck that feeds on fish. Its meat, therefore, has a strong flavor.

2 *poule d'eaux*, cleaned and skinned, head and feet removed
Salt
Ground black pepper
Cayenne pepper
½ cup, plus 3 tablespoons vegetable oil
½ cup all-purpose flour
1 cup chopped onion

½ cup chopped green onion
½ cup finely chopped celery
4 cloves garlic, minced
2 whole bay leaves
2½ quarts unsalted chicken broth or water
¼ pound ham or smoked sausage, minced
Hot cooked rice for serving

1. Wash *poule d'eaux* with cool water. Place in a large pot and cover with water. Add 1 teaspoon salt. Bring to a boil. Lower heat and simmer 5 minutes. Remove ducks, drain, and pat dry. Cut into serving-sized pieces. Season lightly with salt, black pepper, and cayenne pepper.
2. Heat 3 tablespoons oil over medium-high heat in a Dutch oven. Brown duck parts and remove from pot. Leave the fond, the browned bits, in the Dutch oven.
3. In the same pot, heat ½ cup oil over medium flame. Stir in flour and cook, stirring constantly, to form a dark brown roux. Add onion, green onion, celery, garlic, and bay leaves. Cook 10 minutes, stirring constantly. Add broth, ham, and browned duck. Season to taste with salt, black pepper, and cayenne pepper.
4. Bring to a boil. Reduce heat and simmer until birds are tender, about 1 hour. Remove bay leaves. Serve gumbo in individual bowls over hot cooked rice.

Garden Fresh Vegetable Beef Soup

Makes 10–12 servings

This was a family favorite that my mother served with buttery grilled cheese sandwiches or fresh butter and crackers. Mom always made this soup with carrots, corn, potatoes, turnips, celery, onions, and peas. Toward the end of cooking, she would toss in a knot or two of vermicelli and shredded cabbage. You can make this recipe with any of your family's favorite vegetables. To make it vegetarian or vegan, use vegetable broth and omit the meat.

2–2½ pounds beef soup meat or chuck roast, with bone
1 gallon water
1 cup chopped onion
½ cup chopped celery
2 medium potatoes, cubed
4 ounces or more tomato sauce
2 cups shredded cabbage
1 turnip, diced

1 cup each fresh, frozen, or canned green beans and whole-kernel corn
1 cup sliced fresh carrots
1 cup small green peas, frozen or canned
6 ounces vermicelli
Salt and pepper to taste

1. Chop meat into bite-sized chunks and place it and the bone in a 10-quart pot. Add the water, onion, and celery and bring to a boil. Lower heat and simmer until meat is tender, about 1½ hours.
2. Skim top of soup with a small strainer. Add potatoes and tomato sauce. Bring back to a boil and lower to a simmer. When potatoes are half-cooked, after about 15 minutes, add remaining vegetables. Simmer until vegetables are tender, about 15 more minutes.
3. Add vermicelli and gently simmer until pasta is tender. Season soup with salt and pepper. Serve hot.

Swiss Cheese and Ham Soup

Makes 8 servings

Perhaps due to his German heritage, my dad loved Swiss cheese. And we all loved ham served any way. Mom always bought a whole smoked ham, which she boiled, even though it was cooked. She sliced some for sandwiches and used chunks of it for flavoring vegetables. The bone went into a pot of beans or peas. The bits and pieces that clung to the bone, which we call seasoning ham, worked well in this quick soup.

3 cups cubed seasoning ham or
   regular smoked ham
5 cups water
4 tablespoons (½ stick) unsalted
   butter
¼ cup all-purpose flour
1 tablespoon instant minced onion,
   or 2 tablespoons fresh
1 tablespoon instant chicken
   bouillon

4 cups shredded Swiss cheese,
   divided
2 cups half-and-half
2 egg yolks, slightly beaten
¼ teaspoon freshly grated nutmeg
Salt and ground black pepper to taste
8 slices toasted French bread

1. Place ham in a 5-quart pot. Cover with water and bring to a boil. Lower to a simmer and cook 15 minutes. Scoop out ham and reserve ham and broth.
2. Preheat a broiler. Mix butter and flour in a large, heavy-bottomed saucepan. Cook over medium heat, stirring constantly, until bubbly and lightly browned, about 2 minutes. Add onion, bouillon, reserved ham broth, and reserved ham.
3. Stir well and bring to a boil. Lower heat and cook until liquid thickens. Stir in 2 cups cheese, half-and-half, egg yolks, and nutmeg. Simmer 5 minutes.
4. Add salt and pepper to taste. Divide soup among 8 ovenproof bowls. Top each with 1 slice French bread. Sprinkle remaining cheese on bread. Place under hot broiler a few minutes to melt cheese. Serve hot.

Pumpkin Tasso Soup

Makes 6 servings

After Halloween, we enjoyed our jack-o-lanterns as preserves, cookies, and pies. Food was never wasted at our house, so we certainly weren't going to throw out perfectly good pumpkins.

This recipe has become one of my family's favorites. It's flavored with tasso, a spicy version of ham. My family did not make tasso at our *boucherie*, our annual pig butchering, but it was easy to find at the store. If you have trouble finding tasso, you can substitute ham, along with a little extra-hot pepper. To make this soup vegetarian, omit the tasso. For vegan, use a vegetable-based spread or oil in place of butter, and vegetable broth in place of cream. This soup can be made with boiled and mashed sweet potatoes or carrots in place of pumpkin.

1 tablespoon unsalted butter
½ cup chopped onion
1½ teaspoons fresh thyme
3 cups steamed or baked pumpkin, sweet potato, or carrot puree
3 cups chicken broth

½ pound chopped tasso or fried bacon
½ teaspoon salt
¼ teaspoon cayenne or black pepper
¼ teaspoon ground allspice
¼ teaspoon freshly grated nutmeg
1 cup half-and-half

1. Melt butter over medium-high heat in a 5-quart soup pot. Add onion and thyme. Cook until onions are translucent, about 10 minutes.
2. Add pumpkin, broth, and tasso. Bring to a boil, reduce heat, and simmer 20 minutes. Stir in salt, pepper, allspice, and nutmeg.
3. Whisk in half-and-half. Simmer 2 minutes. If you prefer a creamy soup, cool slightly, then puree in a blender and reheat. If soup becomes too thick, thin with broth or half-and-half.

Mirliton Soup

Makes 10 servings

My cousin Valerie first introduced me to this soup. She makes it with shrimp and crabmeat, but it is equally good made with smoked sausage. Mirlitons are green, pear-shaped squash, and my dad grew them in his garden. When his plants did not produce, he would get some from someone in the community. We traditionally had shrimp-stuffed mirlitons for Thanksgiving, as did most everyone else in our village.

8 mirlitons
½ cup (1 stick) unsalted butter or
    olive oil
2 cups diced onion
1½ cups chopped celery
3 green onions, chopped
2 teaspoons minced garlic

¼ cup all-purpose flour
1 whole bay leaf
2–3 quarts chicken or seafood broth
2 cups shrimp, peeled and deveined
½ cup chopped parsley
Salt and pepper to taste
Hot corn bread for serving

1. Place mirlitons in a large pot and cover with water. Boil, uncovered, until just tender, about 30 minutes. Drain and cool. Scoop pulp from shell and discard shell. Finely chop or mash pulp and set aside.
2. Heat butter in a Dutch oven over medium flame. Add onion, celery, green onions, and garlic. Cook until onion is translucent, about 5 minutes. Add mirliton pulp, flour, and bay leaf. Mix well.
3. Gradually whisk in 2 quarts broth. Bring to a boil, reduce heat, and simmer until slightly thickened, about 30 minutes.
4. Add shrimp and parsley. Cook until shrimp turn pink, about 4 minutes. Season to taste with salt and black pepper. If soup is too thick, thin it gradually with remaining stock. Remove bay leaf. Serve hot with corn bread on the side.

Turtle Soup
Makes 12 servings

My uncle Emile was the fisherman of the family. When I was a child, one night he and his friends appeared at my grandmother's house with a large turtle, the prize catch of a fishing expedition. Although my grandmother, mother, and brothers loved turtle soup, we children turned up our noses at the suggestion of eating such a thing. Our sneaky parents cut the meat into a variety of shapes, and we devoured it thinking we were eating fried shrimp and fish.

My friend Melba Champagne says she always thought it was a special treat to have the sandy-textured eggs of turtles cooked in turtle soup. Turtle eggs look like smooth Ping-Pong balls, and Melba's father dug them up along the banks of Bayou des Allemands. People also picked turtle eggs from the banks of Boutte Pond and Bayou Gauche. Boutte Pond was fenced to keep turtles in, but sometimes they got out. When someone butchered a turtle and found eggs inside, those eggs were also often cooked. At Melba's house, the turtle eggs that didn't end up in soup were soft-boiled. Melba and her siblings would tap a hole in each shell and suck out the insides. Some people make mock turtle soup with beef. Melba believes that the addition of turtle eggs proves that there's real turtle in the soup.

3 pounds turtle meat
1¾ cups vegetable oil, divided
1 cup all-purpose flour
2 cups chopped onion
1 cup chopped celery
½ cup chopped bell pepper
3 cloves garlic, minced
3 quarts beef stock or water
4 cups tomato sauce
2 teaspoons salt

½ teaspoon ground bay leaf,
   or 2 whole bay leaves
½ teaspoon ground black pepper
¼ teaspoon cayenne pepper
5 green onions, chopped
2 lemons, thinly sliced
½ cup chopped parsley
½ cup sherry (optional)
Raw turtle eggs or chicken eggs
   (optional)
Louisiana-style hot sauce

1. Remove cartilage, gristle, and silver skin from turtle meat. Cut into ½-inch cubes. Heat ¾ cup vegetable oil in a large skillet over medium-high heat until hot but not smoking and cook turtle meat until brown. Set browned meat aside.
2. In a Dutch oven set over medium heat, make a very dark roux by cooking remaining 1 cup oil and flour together, stirring constantly. Add onion, celery, bell pepper, and garlic. Cook until onion is translucent, about 3 minutes.

3. Stir in stock and tomato sauce. Add salt, bay leaf, black pepper, cayenne pepper, and browned turtle meat. Simmer until meat is tender, about 1½ hours. Soup should cook down to about 3½ quarts.
4. Add green onions, lemon slices, parsley, sherry, and whole eggs. Simmer an additional 15 minutes, or hard-boil and chop eggs, adding to soup just before serving. Season to taste with hot sauce.

Red Bean Gumbo

Makes 4 servings

Soupy red beans cooked with a roux is called red bean gumbo, and it's a dish that's especially popular in neighboring St. James Parish. This recipe is for a shortcut gumbo made with canned beans, which are already thick, and it doesn't call for roux.

2 slices bacon
3 tablespoons all-purpose flour
½ cup finely chopped onion
1 clove garlic, finely chopped
¼ cup chopped ham, or ¼ cup
    smoked andouille, casing removed
    and chopped

1 (27-ounce) can red beans
1 tablespoon chopped parsley
1 whole bay leaf
1 cup meat broth or water
Salt, pepper, or Creole seasoning
Hot cooked rice and buttered French
    bread for serving

1. In a large saucepan over medium-high heat, fry bacon to render fat. Remove bacon. Stir in flour and cook until copper in color, about 4 minutes. Add onion and garlic and cook 3 minutes, stirring constantly.
2. Add bacon, ham, beans, parsley, bay leaf, and broth. Simmer until soup is just starting to get creamy, but not too thick, about 15 minutes.
3. Adjust seasoning to taste, using salt, pepper, or Creole seasoning. Remove bay leaf. For creamy bean gumbo, cool beans slightly, then puree in a blender. Serve gumbo hot over rice and with a side of hot buttered French bread.

2

The Boucherie

THE FIRST COLD SPELL of winter on the German Coast meant that the pig that had been living all year in a pen in the backyard was now going to provide some seasonal delicacies. Early in the morning, the men in the family would gather in the backyard to get ready for the *boucherie*, the pig butchering. The first thing they did was put my grandfather's big black iron pot over an open fire and fill it with water. Lots of hot water was needed to "shave the pig" of its coarse bristles.

While the water was heating, the men put fine edges on their knives with a sharpening steel or Papaul's leather strap, the whole while enjoying hot café au lait and biscuits with homemade fig preserves and butter. After a makeshift table was made from carpenter horses and strong planks, the pig's throat was slit with a sharp knife, and the carcass was laid on the table. (One year, a neighbor rushed from her house to warn my pregnant sister that if she watched the boucherie proceedings her baby would be born with a pig-shaped birthmark. For the record: she did watch, and her son had no birthmark.)

The women would ready the kitchen for making all sorts of delicious pork specialties. White boudin is a pig's intestine stuffed with a mixture of well-seasoned rice and ground pork and liver. Red boudin, also called blood boudin, is made with pig's blood. The ladies in my family also made hogshead cheese, a terrine of seasoned bits of pork, as well as cracklins, which we called *gratons*. (Cracklins/*gratons* are not the same as pork skins.) No boucherie was complete without the production of sausages, including fresh sausage and smoked andouille.

Back in those days, we had only gas space heaters to warm the house. On boucherie day, my grandmother kept the living room cold because this is where she would place the hogshead cheese to gel. Andouille was smoked with pecan wood in a makeshift smoker in the backyard near the fig trees, then hung on the back porch rafters until it was needed for a Sunday gumbo.

For lunch on boucherie day, the women made grits and grillades with braised bits and pieces of the fresh pork. Everyone went home with a "pockay" (package) of meat.

The marriage of German and French cuisines on the German Coast resulted in the development of many foods, such as andouille, fresh hot sausage, hogshead cheese, boudin, and various cured meats.

Andouille
Makes 4 pounds sausage

I once made a trek to sixteen different stores that make andouille, starting in LaPlace and going west through Lafayette, then doubling back and heading over to New Orleans. My conclusion is that the LaPlace style of andouille, which is coarser, leaner, and more heavily smoked than that made in other parts of the state, is reflective of robust German cuisine. Southwest Louisiana's andouille—which is lightly smoked, contains tripe, and is more peppery—is more delicate, like French preparations.

4½ pounds pork butt
½ pound pork fat
5 teaspoons salt
2 teaspoons black pepper

2 teaspoons garlic powder
1 teaspoon cayenne pepper
5–6 feet of 2-inch beef or pork
  sausage casing

1. Cut pork and fat into ½-inch cubes. Place in a large bowl, add seasonings, and mix well. Cover and refrigerate for several hours or overnight.
2. Tie off one end of the sausage casing. Using an extremely clean mechanical sausage stuffer, stuff the chilled, seasoned meat into the open end of the casing. When the casing is filled, twist the sausages about every 6 inches in alternating directions to make links. Twist the open end and tie with string.
3. Smoke your chain of links using pecan or hickory wood at low temperature (175–200°F) for 4–5 hours, or until the casing is dark and the meat is thoroughly cooked. Finished temperature should be 170°F. Cool and wrap andouille in several layers of aluminum foil; it will keep in the freezer indefinitely.

Fresh Deer Sausage
Makes 20 pounds

This recipe was passed down from my uncle Ernest Keller, better known as Gee Gee, who gave it to someone in the family, who gave it to my friend Dale, who gave it to me. Purportedly, this is a near-duplication of the sausage that was famously made for many years at the now-closed Hahnville Mercantile grocery store. I later got the original Hahnville Mercantile recipe, which is made with pork and beef. That recipe follows this one.

20 pounds coarsely ground deer
    meat
5 pounds ground pork
4 cups cold water
6 tablespoons salt
3 tablespoons ground black pepper

3 tablespoons garlic powder
3 tablespoons ground thyme
3 tablespoons onion powder
2 tablespoons cayenne pepper
2 tablespoons celery flakes

1. Mix together ground deer meat, pork, and cold water. Spread meat on a clean surface and pat into a 2-inch-thick rectangle. Sprinkle seasonings evenly over meat and mix with your hands. Place in a large bowl, cover, and refrigerate overnight.
2. Grind meat again and form into a rectangle. Roll jellyroll style, then mix thoroughly with your hands. If you have a commercial 36-quart mixer, you can put the seasoned meat into the mixer bowl and mix on low speed until seasoning is well incorporated.
3. Make patties using ¼ cup of mixture for each. Mixture can also be stuffed into sausage casings.
4. Freeze patties on a metal pan and transfer to plastic freezer bags for freezer storage. To cook, heat a heavy-bottomed skillet over high heat. Fry sausage patties or links on all sides until completely cooked through, about 4 minutes per side for patties. Drain and serve hot.

Note: This sausage makes good meatloaf and tamales. It can also be made with a combination of 50 percent deer meat and 50 percent ground pork or a higher-fat-content beef. Fatty meat is needed because venison is lean, and without fat from other meats the sausage would be dry.

Hahnville Mercantile Fresh Pork Sausage

Makes 15 pounds

This is the original recipe for Hahnville Mercantile's famous sausage. It was given to me by Bert Songy, who got it from Amedee Keller's daughter after Mr. Amedee died. Mr. Amedee was the store's original owner, and everyone just called the store Amedee's.

10 pounds coarsely ground pork
5 pounds coarsely ground beef
2–3 quarts water
½ cup salt

2 tablespoons garlic powder
2 tablespoons red pepper
1 tablespoon onion powder

Mix as directed in the recipe for Fresh Deer Sausage on page 24. I find that using 3 quarts water works best.

Cracklins

Makes about 2½ pounds

My German grandfather Papaul kept up the tradition of the annual boucherie. The family boucheries were always held at his house. The day of the boucherie, Mémère had to hide freshly made cracklins from the children, or there would not be enough for homemade bread for the big family supper that night. We loved snacking on cracklins and added them to grits, biscuits, and cornbread. We used the rendered lard in just about every pastry we baked.

5 pounds cold pork skin, with fat,
    preferably with bits of meat
1 pint water or oil

Salt
Cayenne pepper or Creole seasoning

1. Dice fat into 1½-inch chunks. Place water in a large, deep, black iron pot. Add pork. Bring to a boil and cook on medium heat until fat is rendered and meat is brown, tender, and crisp, about 1 hour.
2. Drain cracklins and season with salt and cayenne pepper or your favorite Creole seasoning. Store in a covered container in the refrigerator.

Blood (Red) Boudin

Makes 3 pounds sausage

As a child, I loved fried blood boudin with grits for breakfast. When I grew older and realized I was eating coagulated blood, I got a little squeamish, but eventually I got over that.

To get that blood, a sharp knife is quickly inserted into the main artery of the pig's neck. After the pig stops moving, it is laid down on a table and scrubbed, rinsed, and shaved. A knife is stuck back into a main neck artery, and the pig's blood is carefully caught in a large clean bowl, pot, or bucket, in which the salt and pepper has already been placed. My cousin Morris Hymel (we all call him Rooster) still occasionally makes blood boudin. Rooster gave me this recipe, which he will hand down to his son. This is as close as I can get to my grandfather Leopold's recipe for blood boudin. Rooster shared this bit of boucherie history about his recipe:

"This is the recipe handed down from my father, Willie Hymel Sr. This recipe has been in the family forever. My son Douglas Hymel will have this recipe, and hopefully he will pass it on to the next generation. First, whenever Dad would make a 'boucherie,' it was a family gathering. It was always scheduled on one of the coldest days, normally in January. There wasn't much to do in the fields at this time of the year, so this was an ideal time to kill a hog since there were many family members available to help. Just about everything was used from the hog except the squeal and the hair. Red boudin was made from the blood of the hog. This is called black pudding in Ireland, France, and Germany and is often served at breakfast, just as we do here."

4 tablespoons salt	2 teaspoons ground black pepper
6 cups pork blood from a freshly butchered pig (instructions follow)	½ cup chopped green onions
	¼ cup finely chopped garlic
	4 tablespoons chopped parsley
Pork fat from the pig's neck (instructions follow)	1 cup cooked white rice
	Sausage casing and cotton kitchen
½ cup lard or water	string or dental floss

1. Place salt in a large cooking pot. Bleed a hog that has been scrubbed, scraped, and doused with scalding hot water into the pot. While bleeding the hog, keep stirring the blood with the salt to keep it from clabbering. It should take about 5 minutes to bleed the hog. Set the pot of blood aside.

2. Cut the pig's skin along with the fat from under the neck. This should yield about 1½–2 pounds of fat. Trim the fat from the skin. Cut the fat into ¼–¾-inch pieces.
3. Place about ½ cup lard or water in a large, heavy pot. Place fat chunks in the pot and fry until the fat is rendered out. You now have cracklins, which should be soft. Remove cracklins from the pot and drain. (You can crisp them up later.) Reserve fat in the pot.
4. After the fat left in the pot has cooled, add blood with salt, and pepper. Add green onions, garlic, and parsley.
5. Add rice. Stir mixture with a wire whisk to break up any clabbered blood. Adjust the seasoning. (Usually, the boldest and most experienced man in the group does this.)
6. Tie one end of the casing with cotton string. Fill 18–21 inches of casing using a boudinier, a funnel-like device that holds the casing open while being filled, or use a sausage stuffer or the sausage-stuffing attachment on a meat grinder or food processor. After the casing is full, tie the open end with string. Leave the string ends about 10 inches long. Repeat process with any remaining boudin filling.
7. Place a glass pie dish in the bottom of a large pot to keep the boudin from sticking to the bottom of the pot. Fill the pot halfway with cold water. Place the filled casings in the pot. Be sure that the casings are covered with water.
8. Turn the burner under the pot to medium heat. When steam starts rising from the water, turn the heat to low. Cook on low 2½–3 hours. (Higher heat will cause the boudin to burst, and you will have a mess and no boudin.)
9. To test if the boudin is cooked, take hold of the long string, lift the boudin out of the water, and stick it with a toothpick. If no liquid oozes out, the boudin is cooked. If liquid comes out, submerge boudin back into the water and continue cooking a few more minutes.
10. Cooked temperature should be around 158°F. Set cooked boudin on towels to dry. Cool. To serve, grill or fry. This sausage also freezes well.

White Boudin

Makes 6 pounds sausage

This is a fresh sausage made with pork liver and pork meat, along with seasonings. The authoritative French cookbook *Larousse Gastronomique* states that rice is an essential part of French boudins, both red and white. Some local recipes don't call for rice, so I suppose that is a German influence. Some people make theirs with barley, which, to me, would indicate an Irish touch, and we did have Irish families in the area. My family did not add rice to this sausage filling, although others, especially in southwestern Louisiana, did. Since a boucherie only produced one liver, there was never a lot of white boudin, and every little piece was considered a treat.

4 pounds pork liver
2 pounds pork butt, bone-in
3 onions
3 stalks celery
1 head garlic, cloves peeled

⅓ cup chopped parsley
2 tablespoons salt
2 teaspoons ground black pepper
½ teaspoon cayenne pepper
4 feet pork or beef casing

1. Place all ingredients except casing in a large boiling pot. Cover with water and bring to a boil. Lower heat and simmer until liver is tender, about 1½ hours. Remove liver from pot. Cool and break into chunks.
2. Meanwhile, continue cooking pork butt until tender, about another 30 minutes. Drain and reserve seasoning vegetables and 1 cup liquid. Cool and remove meat from bone and cut into chunks. Coarse-grind liver and pork. Discard vegetable skins, and coarse-grind seasoning vegetables. Mix ground vegetables with meat mixture and 1 cup of reserved liquid. Season with additional salt and pepper if desired.
3. Stuff boudin into casing using a boudinier, a funnel-like device that holds the casing open while being filled, or use a sausage stuffer or the sausage-stuffing attachment on a meat grinder or food processor. Twist off links by twisting or tying.
4. To cook, heat a large pot of water to 190°F. Add sausage and cook, uncovered, 25–30 minutes. Do not allow to boil since boiling will increase the risk of the casing splitting. Cool, then refrigerate or freeze.

Hogshead Cheese

Makes 8 pounds

There are no dairy products in this "cheese," which is a molded pork gelatin often served as an appetizer. The old folks called hogshead cheese *la gelée* (pronounced la ge-lay). Mam Papaul placed her hogshead cheese in her cold living room to jell. Most of it was taken home by family and friends who had helped with the boucherie.

Back then, hogshead cheese was made with pig feet gelatin and actual hogs' heads. Modern recipes typically use pork butt in place of a hog's head meat and commercial gelatin in place of pig feet.

6 pounds pork butt
1½ quarts water or meat stock
3 cups finely chopped onions
3 cups finely chopped celery
20 cloves garlic, minced
2 tablespoons salt

1 teaspoon ground bay leaf, or
  2 fresh leaves
1 teaspoon dried thyme leaves
1 teaspoon ground black pepper
½ teaspoon cayenne pepper
½ cup chopped parsley
7 envelopes unflavored gelatin

1. Place all ingredients except gelatin in a large stock pot and cover with water. Bring to a boil, then reduce heat, cover, and simmer until meat is very tender, about 2 hours. Skim top of pot and discard. Drain meat and discard bones, reserving stock and cooked vegetables. Chop meat coarsely and set aside.
2. Sprinkle gelatin over 2 cups cool water. Let stand 3 minutes. In a large pot, heat reserved stock to just a simmer and remove from heat. Stir in gelatin mixture. In a separate large bowl, combine chopped pork and cooked seasoning vegetables with 1½ quarts gelatin mixture. Adjust seasoning to taste.
3. Place meat mixture into loaf pans or molds, leaving 1½ inches head space. Cover tops with 1 inch of gelatin mixture.
4. Place molds in refrigerator overnight to gel. Unmold the cheese and serve on crackers as an appetizer or snack. Hogshead cheese can be frozen, but it will have to be melted on the stove and regelled in the refrigerator.

Boston Butt Cheese

Makes 26 (1-pound) chunks

This recipe was given to me by my uncle Joe's nephew Bert "Dudda" Songy. Uncle Joe and his eight siblings grew up in Edgard, on the German Coast. This recipe contains liver, so it's a little different from my grandmother Mam Papaul's version. Veal knuckle bones provide plenty of gelatin, so you won't need commercial gelatin.

10 pounds pork Boston butt, cut into ½-inch pieces
6 pounds pork skin, cut into 1- and 2-inch pieces
3 veal knuckle bones
8 bay leaves
½ cup salt

⅓ cup Worcestershire sauce
⅓ cup Tabasco-brand pepper sauce
¼ cup red pepper
¼ cup black pepper
3 pounds pork liver, cut into ¼-inch cubes
Crackers for serving

1. Place all ingredients except liver in a large pot and cover with water. Stir well to distribute peppers and dissolve salt.
2. Bring to a boil. Lower heat and simmer until meat and skin are tender, about 2–2½ hours.
3. Add liver and simmer until liver is cooked through, about 20 minutes.
4. Remove bay leaves and veal knuckle bones. Remove meat from bones and return it to mixture; discard bones. Spoon mixture evenly into molds. Chill until firm. Serve as an appetizer with crackers.

Stuffed Ponce

Makes 6 servings

Ponce is a pig's stomach stuffed with seasoned meat, a Cajun specialty some-times called *chaudin*. Today, stuffed ponce is mostly found in meat shops in southwestern Louisiana. My mama became friends with a neighbor who worked for a butcher, and she was thrilled when she could get a ponce for boiling, stuffing, or frying. It came straight from the slaughterhouse, and she spent hours by the cistern cleaning it.

1 (1-pound) pig stomach (ponce)
1¾ pounds lean ground pork
¾ cup finely chopped onion
3 green onions, finely chopped
1 stalk celery, finely chopped
3¼ cups water
1½ cups raw rice
1 medium sweet potato, peeled and finely chopped in a food processor

1 stick unsalted butter, melted
¼ cup finely chopped parsley
1 tablespoon salt
¼ teaspoon black pepper
¼ teaspoon cayenne pepper
1 medium green apple, seeded and halved

1. Clean, scrape, and soak the ponce in cold water for 1 hour.
2. Preheat oven to 350°F. Brown ground pork in a deep pan or Dutch oven. Add onion, green onions, and celery. Cook over low heat until onion is soft, approximately 8 minutes. Add remaining ingredients except apple. Stir well. Bring to a boil, reduce heat, cover, and simmer until rice has absorbed the liquid and is tender, approximately 20 minutes. Cool on a rimmed baking sheet.
3. Tie one end of the ponce with string or dental floss to form a pouch. Press an apple half inside the tied end of the ponce. Fill the ponce with stuffing. Place the other apple half in the open end of the stuffed ponce. Close the opening by tying or sewing the string. (If you have too much stuffing, heat in a microwave oven at medium power and serve separately. Check stuffing during cooking; microwave power settings vary in temperature.)
4. Place stuffed ponce in a rimmed baking pan with 1 cup water. Bake, un-covered, until ponce is nicely browned and crisp, about 1 hour. Let stand 20 minutes before slicing.

Cochon de Lait
(Roasted Suckling Pig)
Makes 20 servings

Cochon de lait is the French term for a small milk-fed pig. Today, any size pig cooked outdoors is referred to as a *cochon de lait*. The event is also referred to as a *cochon de lait*.

1 (25–35-pound) suckling pig
Plenty of hot and cold water
2 pounds bacon fat or lard
¾ cup salt

⅓ cup ground black pepper
¼ cup ground cayenne pepper
4 tablespoons powdered garlic
Ice to cover bottom of a cooler

Stuffing

4 pounds seasoned bulk sausage
2 cups chopped onion
2 cups chopped celery
2 cups finely chopped green bell
    pepper
4 cups fresh bread crumbs made
    from French bread

1 cup apple juice
4 teaspoons Worcestershire sauce
2 teaspoons thyme
1 teaspoon oregano or sage (optional)
Salt and black pepper to taste

For baking and presentation:

2 cups boiling water
4 tablespoons butter
1 small red apple or orange

2 slices carrot
Fresh fruit and edible greens for
    garnish

1. Wash pig. Pour hot water all over pig. Scrape off bristles with a sharp knife. Wash again with cool water and drain by hanging upside down.
2. Use a clean cloth to pat pig dry inside and out. Puncture inside of the pig at 4-inch intervals, being careful not to go through the skin. Mix bacon fat with salt, black pepper, cayenne pepper, and garlic. Rub inside of pig with this mixture. Place ice in a large cooler. Cover ice with heavy-duty aluminum foil. Place seasoned pig on ice; cover with another layer aluminum foil. Keep cooler closed until ready to stuff and roast pig. Let marinate at least 6 hours.

3. To make stuffing: In a large skillet, brown the sausage; add onion, celery, and bell pepper. Cook until onions are translucent. Add bread crumbs, apple juice, Worcestershire sauce, thyme, oregano, salt, and pepper. Mix well.
4. Stuff pig with stuffing mixture. Sew or tie back end closed. Fold front legs together and tie underneath the pig. Fold back legs together and tie.
5. Preheat oven to 350°F. Place pig on its belly in a large baking pan. Remove head if whole pig does not fit in pan; place head and body in different pans to bake. Place a large wad of aluminum foil in the pig's mouth to hold it open. Cover pig loosely with parchment paper and place in oven. Mix boiling water with butter. For the next 3 hours, baste both the pig and the parchment paper every half hour with butter and water mixture. (Make additional butter/water mixture, if needed.)
6. Remove parchment after 3 hours. Bake an additional 3 hours to brown and crisp the skin. Finished temperature should be 160–170°F.
7. Slide a durable plastic chopping board or a rimless baking sheet under pig and remove it to a serving platter. Replace foil in pig's mouth with an apple or orange. Place head onto body on platter. Place carrot slices in eye sockets. Garnish neckline where head and body come together with fruit and greens. Place on buffet or serving table for all to view before carving. Slice and serve. Chop leftovers for pulled-pork sandwiches.

Converted Rice Jambalaya for a Crowd

Makes 150 servings

This recipe is good for large crowds, and it's often prepared outdoors over a propane burner.

1 pint vegetable oil
25 pounds parboiled/converted rice
10 pounds onions, chopped
10 large bell peppers, seeded and chopped
4 bunches celery, chopped
5 cups chopped green onions
6 heads garlic, peeled and chopped
3 bunches parsley, chopped
25 pounds smoked pork sausage, sliced

5 pounds ground beef
2 gallons water or unseasoned broth
1 gallon tomato sauce
1 (5-ounce) bottle Worcestershire sauce
5½ ounces Creole seasoning
6 tablespoons salt
4 tablespoons ground black pepper

1. In the biggest heavy-bottomed pot you can find, heat oil over medium-high heat and cook rice until the grains turn white. Add onions, bell peppers, celery, green onions, garlic, and parsley. Cook 10 minutes, stirring constantly.
2. Add sausage and ground beef and cook 15 minutes. Stir in water, tomato sauce, Worcestershire sauce, Creole seasoning, salt, and pepper. Bring to a boil. Stir and cover tightly. Lower heat and cook until rice is tender. This may take 2 or more hours, depending on the type of pot you're using. Serve hot.

Paneéd Meat with White Gravy

Makes 6 servings

What we call *paneéd* meat in south Louisiana is known as chicken fried steak in Texas, and schnitzel in Germany. In Germany, the meat is typically served with a béchamel sauce laced with wine. Here we make this same sauce without wine and call it white sauce or white gravy.

6 (4-ounce) veal, pork, or chicken
   cutlets
1 cup all-purpose flour
1 teaspoon salt
½ teaspoon ground black pepper

2 large eggs
6 tablespoons water
Vegetable oil for frying
White Sauce (Gravy) for serving
   (*recipe follows*)

1. Pound meat to ¼-inch thickness. In a shallow bowl, mix flour, salt, and pepper. In a separate small bowl, whisk egg with water. Dredge cutlets in the seasoned flour, then dip in the egg wash, then dredge again in the flour.
2. Heat 1 inch oil in a deep skillet to 325°F. Fry breaded cutlets on each side until lightly browned, about 3 minutes per side. Serve warm with White Sauce.

White Sauce (Gravy)

Makes 1½ cups

4 tablespoons (½ stick) unsalted
   butter
3 tablespoons all-purpose flour

1½ cups milk
Salt, pepper, and nutmeg or mace
   to taste

1. Melt butter in a 2-quart saucepan. Stir in flour and cook on low heat for 3 minutes, stirring often.
2. Raise heat to medium and whisk in milk, salt, pepper, and nutmeg. Continue whisking until all lumps have disappeared.
3. Cook on low heat, stirring constantly, until thick and bubbly, about 5 minutes. Keep warm until ready to use.

Fried Pork Chops

Makes 6 servings

At our house, pork chops were always served with white beans and rice. For a delicious fried pork chop sandwich, remove the bone and slip the cooked meat between two slices of bread.

6 (4-ounce) center-cut, ½-inch-thick
   pork chops
1½ teaspoons salt
¼ teaspoon ground black pepper

¼ teaspoon cayenne pepper
½ cup vegetable oil
¼ cup water

1. Rinse pork chops with cool water. Pat dry and season with salt, black pepper, and cayenne pepper.
2. Heat oil in a large skillet until it reaches 350°F. Fry pork chops until lightly browned on each side, or until the inside temperature reaches 140°F. Remove from pan and keep warm on a covered plate.
3. Pour most of the oil out of pan and discard. Add water to remaining drippings and bring to a fast simmer. Stir constantly, scraping bottom of skillet to make a thin gravy. Serve gravy over pork chops. (Sometimes we serve the gravy with grits and make sandwiches with the pork chops.)

Grits and Grillades

Makes 4–6 servings

This was one of our boucherie-day dishes, and it's a simple recipe made with scraps of pork simmered in a brown gravy and served over grits. We flavored grillades with whatever seasoning vegetables were available, such as onions or green onions. (We call green onions "shallots.")

1 (1½-pound) pork tenderloin, cut into cubes or thinly sliced
1¼ teaspoons salt
½ teaspoon ground black pepper
Cayenne pepper to taste
⅓ cup all-purpose flour
5 tablespoons vegetable oil

½ cup chopped onion
½ cup chopped green onions
¼ cup chopped bell pepper
2 cloves garlic, minced
3 cups water or meat broth
2 tablespoons chopped parsley
Hot grits for serving (*recipe follows*)

1. To make grillades, season pork with salt, black pepper, and cayenne pepper. Roll meat in flour. Over medium-high heat, heat oil in a large, heavy skillet or pot until hot. Brown pork in oil and set aside. Cook fond—the crust that has formed at the bottom of the skillet—to deep brown.
2. Add onion, green onions, bell pepper, and garlic to skillet. Cook 6 minutes, stirring occasionally. Add water and simmer briskly, stirring well and scraping bottom of skillet to dissolve the brown bits.
3. Return pork to the skillet. Cover and cook on medium heat until pork is tender and gravy is slightly thick, about 30 minutes. Stir in parsley. Serve grillades and gravy over grits.

Grits

Makes 4–6 servings

4 cups water or milk
1 teaspoon salt
1 cup quick grits

¼ teaspoon ground black pepper
2 tablespoons unsalted butter
(optional)

Bring water and salt to a boil in a medium saucepan. Reduce heat to a simmer. Slowly add grits, stirring constantly. Cover and cook 5 minutes on low heat, or follow directions on grits package. Add pepper and butter. Serve hot.

Stuffed Cabbage

Makes 8 servings

Storks delivered babies in cabbage patches on the German Coast—at least that's what I was told. I remember checking the sky when my younger sister Dale was born. Judging by the large size of the region's typical family, those storks must have come by often.

My German mother did not make cabbage rolls, nor did she cook her cabbage in tomato sauce or juice, as did most Germans. But she did stuff whole cabbages, and when one appeared on the table, we practically licked the serving platter clean. To keep her cabbage from falling apart, Mom tied it together with string. When I make her recipe, I simply put the stuffed cabbage in a foil-covered stainless steel bowl and bake it. A Dutch oven works as well, but my huge stuffed cabbages do not fit in my smallish cast-iron Dutch oven.

1 medium (2–2½-pound) leafy cabbage	¾ cup raw long-grain rice
½ pound ground beef	1½ cups water
½ pound ground bulk pork	1 teaspoon salt
¼ cup finely chopped onion	½ teaspoon ground black pepper
¼ cup finely chopped green onions	½ teaspoon powdered bay leaf
¼ cup finely chopped celery	4 (20-inch) pieces of cotton string
1 clove garlic, minced	½ cup (1 stick) butter, melted

1. Pull 4 large, heavy leaves from the head of cabbage and set aside. Place the whole cabbage head in a 5-quart Dutch oven and cover with water. Remove cabbage and bring water to boil. Add whole cabbage and loose leaves to boiling water. Cover pot and boil 12 minutes. Drain and set whole head and separate leaves aside.

2. Push as many leaves as you can away from the inside core, being careful not to detach them. Using a sharp knife, cut a circle deep into the cabbage around the core, but not through the bottom of the cabbage. Remove the core and any leaves that do not easily bend.

3. Preheat oven to 350°F. To make stuffing, add ground beef and pork to a large, heavy skillet set over medium-high heat. Sauté until meat is brown, about 10 minutes. Remove 4 tablespoons of accumulated grease and discard. Add onion, green onions, celery, and garlic. Cook, stirring often, until onion is translucent, about 5 minutes.

4. Add rice and cook, stirring constantly, until rice turns white. Stir in water, salt, pepper, and bay leaf. Bring to a boil. Lower heat to a bare simmer, cover pot, and cook until rice is tender, about 25 minutes.

5. Place a generous amount of meat and rice stuffing between each cabbage leaf and in the core cavity. Cover top of cabbage with reserved leaves. Place strings under the cabbage, spacing them evenly apart. Push cabbage into shape and tie strings on top to secure the leaves.

6. Place stuffed cabbage in a stainless-steel bowl or Dutch oven. Drizzle with melted butter. Bake, covered, until cabbage is golden brown, about 1½ hours. Remove to a platter and serve warm.

Pork Roast

Makes 12 servings

After a boucherie, the garlic lovers in my family looked forward to this savory treat. Leftovers make great shredded-pork poor boy sandwiches. This was one of my mother's favorite dishes.

10-pound pork shoulder roast, bone-in
1 cup finely chopped onion
2½ tablespoons salt
1 tablespoon ground black pepper
1 teaspoon cayenne pepper

20 (1-inch) pieces bacon
20 slivers of garlic
3 tablespoons vegetable oil
1½ cups water, divided
2 tablespoons cornstarch

1. Wash roast with cold water and pat dry with paper towels. Make 20 deep slits in roast.

2. Mix together onion, salt, black pepper, and cayenne pepper. Into each roast slit, stuff 1 piece bacon, 1 sliver garlic, and some of the onion mixture.

3. Preheat oven to 350°F. Rub roast with oil and remaining onion mixture. Heat a roasting pan over a medium-high flame, add roast, and brown well on all sides.

4. Pour ½ cup water in pan. Cover and bake until internal temperature reaches 160°F, about 3¼ hours. Add additional water if needed.

5. Remove roast to a serving platter and cover with aluminum foil. Deglaze roasting pan with ½ cup water. Mix cornstarch with remaining ½ cup water and pour into roasting pan. Stir and cook over medium-high heat until thickened. Adjust seasoning. Serve roast sliced and covered with gravy.

Pig Tails

Makes 4 servings

Believe it or not, when I was a child, this was the most sought after part of the pig. Mama boiled it, and the person lucky enough to get it ate it coated with vinegar-and-oil dressing.

A pig's tail is bony and is a combination of skin and fat. The texture of a cooked one is silky soft, like pickled pig's feet.

4 pig tails
Water
Salt and pepper to taste

½ cup oil
½ cup vinegar

1. Wash and scrape tails well. Place in a large pot and add enough water to cover. Add salt. Bring to a boil, then lower to a simmer. Cook until tails are tender, about 1–1½ hours.
2. To make dressing, whisk together oil and vinegar. Season with salt and pepper. Serve pigtails warm or at room temperature with dressing.

Brains and Onions

Makes 2 servings

This was my grandfather Faucheux's favorite supper the night after a boucherie. My mother and brother loved this dish, too. Mama often added a few beaten eggs to the sautéed brains during the last ten minutes of cooking.

¼ cup butter
½ cup chopped onion
¼ cup chopped green onions
1 tablespoon chopped parsley

1 cup pig brains
2 large eggs, beaten (optional)
Salt and pepper to taste

1. Melt butter over medium heat in a heavy skillet. Add onion, green onions, and parsley. Cook three minutes.
2. Add brains and cook 2 minutes on each side. Add eggs.
3. Continue cooking on low heat until eggs are set, about 10 minutes. Season with salt and pepper and serve hot.

Pork Fricassee (Stew)

Makes 10–12 servings

At first I was going to write that we did not make fricassee, but that is not quite true. We just pronounce the word differently; we say "free-CA-say."

1½ cups all-purpose flour, divided	2½ cups chopped onion
2½ teaspoons salt	1 cup chopped green onions
¼ teaspoon cayenne or ground black pepper	6 cloves garlic, minced
2–3 pounds pork roast, cut into 2-inch cubes	5 cups water or broth
½ cup vegetable oil	2 cups diced carrots or turnips
	¼ cup chopped parsley
	Hot cooked rice for serving

1. In a small, shallow bowl, mix together ½ cup flour, salt, and pepper. Dredge meat in flour mixture. Heat a large, heavy-bottomed saucepan or Dutch oven over medium-high heat and add oil. Brown meat on all sides and set aside.
2. Add remaining cup of flour, lower heat to medium, and stir constantly until the roux you're making is the color of a copper penny. Add onion, green onions, and garlic. Cook 6 minutes, stirring constantly. Add water. Stir well to remove the brown bits clinging to the bottom of the pot.
3. Add meat and bring to a boil. Cover and lower heat to a simmer. After about 1½ hours, meat should be tender and gravy should be beginning to thicken. At this point, add diced carrots. Cover and cook until carrots are tender and gravy is thick, about 20 minutes. Stir in parsley. Adjust seasoning to taste. Serve hot over rice.

Fricassee au Tee Cochon (Little Pig Stew)

Makes 10–12 servings

This stew is made with pig offal, and it was the Acadians who introduced it to the German Coast. This dish was especially popular in St. John the Baptist Parish. My uncle Joe, who grew up in Edgard, said that it was a favorite in his family. To make this stew, use the preceding recipe and omit the carrots or turnips. Add the pork meat and the pig's heart, liver, kidneys, tail, and feet. Uncle Joe said that the children in the family particularly liked the meat and skin from the tail and feet.

Ham-Stuffed Onions

Makes 6 servings

My mama told me that my great-grandmother Mémère Clarice often made this dish for her husband, my great-grandfather Pépère Zoot, who lived to be 102 years old. Pépère Zoot was the father of my grandfather Leopold Faucheux. Mama made this dish only a few times when we were young because, like most children, we did not like the strong taste of onions. Pépère Zoot always had a garden and was known for his green thumb, so fresh vegetables were served at every meal.

6 medium onions
4 tablespoons butter, melted, divided
1 cup finely chopped ham
1 cup soft bread crumbs (made from stale bread)
4 tablespoons chopped green onions
4 tablespoons chopped green bell pepper
½ teaspoon salt
⅛ teaspoon ground black pepper
1¼ cups water or milk
½ cup fine bread crumbs

1. Preheat oven to 375°F. Peel off onion skins. Carefully cut ¼ inch off tops and bottoms of whole onions. (Reserve onion skins for boiling to color Easter eggs.)
2. Bring 2 inches of water to boil in a Dutch oven. Stand onions in boiling water, cover pot, and simmer until onions are just beginning to get tender, about 8–10 minutes. Drain and pull out centers, leaving a ½-inch shell. Reserve onion centers for another use.
3. Add 2 tablespoons melted butter to a skillet set over medium-high heat. Add ham, soft bread crumbs, green onions, bell peppers, salt, and pepper. Stir well. Stuff mixture into onion cups. Stand onions up in a baking dish.
4. Pour water around onions in dish. Mix remaining 2 tablespoons melted butter with bread crumbs and sprinkle over tops of onions. Bake until tops are brown, about 30 minutes or longer for softer texture. Serve warm.

Pork and Oyster Pâté

Makes 6–8 servings

This dish is a pie. I don't know why we call it pâté. All along the German Coast, hot pork and oyster pâté was served with fresh cane syrup. Chef John Folse—who owns several area restaurants, has written several cookbooks, and even cooked in Moscow for Ronald Reagan and Mikhail Gorbachev—grew up in St. James Parish and enjoys pork and oyster paté served with syrup, just as we do.

1 pound ground pork
⅓ cup vegetable oil
⅓ cup all-purpose flour
1 cup chopped onion
4 green onions, with tops, chopped
8 large oysters, chopped
Oyster liquid, plus enough hot water to make 1¾ cups
¼ teaspoon salt

¼ teaspoon ground black pepper
Cayenne pepper to taste
Easy Pastry for Savory Fillings (*recipe follows*), or 2 (9-inch) purchased pie crusts
1 large egg
3 tablespoons water
Cane syrup for serving

1. Preheat oven to 375°F. Brown ground pork over medium-high heat in a skillet. Drain and set aside.
2. In a large, heavy-bottomed saucepan, heat oil over medium heat. Add flour and stir constantly to make a medium-brown (penny-colored) roux. Add onion and continue cooking 8 minutes, stirring constantly.
3. Add green onions, oysters, oyster liquid, salt, black pepper, and cayenne pepper. Cover and cook on low heat until gravy is very thick, approximately 20 minutes. Adjust seasonings. Set aside to cool.
4. Preheat oven to 350°F. Make Easy Pastry for Savory Fillings and cut in half. Roll one-half into an 11-inch circle. Fit rolled pastry into a 9-inch pie pan. Place cooled filling into pastry-lined pan. Roll out second piece of pastry into a 10-inch circle and cover top of pie. Crimp edges and make 3 slits in top of crust with a sharp knife.
5. Make an egg wash by beating egg with water. Brush top of crust with egg wash and bake until golden brown, approximately 45 minutes. Serve hot with cane syrup poured on top.

Easy Pastry for Savory Fillings

Makes 2 (9-inch) pie crusts

3 cups all-purpose flour

1 teaspoon salt

1¼ cups vegetable shortening or lard, chilled

5 tablespoons very cold water

1 tablespoon vinegar

1 large egg

1. In a large bowl, mix flour and salt. Using a pastry blender, cut shortening into flour mixture until it resembles small peas.
2. Mix water, vinegar, and egg together until well blended. Slowly add liquid to flour mixture, mixing well with a spoon to make the dough.
3. Press dough together by placing it on a floured dish towel. Bring ends of towel into center to pull dough together to form a ball.
4. Remove dough from towel and knead 4 or 5 times. Dough is now ready to roll. If dough is not needed immediately, place in a plastic bag and refrigerate.

Pépère Zoot (Charles Faucheux) dozing on the front porch, with his daughter Pauline standing behind him.

BEEF, POULTRY, AND GAME

THE SHELL OIL REFINERY in Norco across the Mississippi River has been our area's primary employer for many years. At the time I was growing up, there was no nearby bridge. A foot ferry ran workers across; rain or shine, night or day, the ferry got them to their jobs. After a day of work, the men came home to more work, such as farming and caring for livestock. The women fed the chickens and put them in the henhouse at night. Although no one on the German Coast owned large herds of cattle or a ranch, each family kept one or two cows that provided milk and, eventually, meat for the table.

A few people also had sheep, as did we at one point. My dad eked out a living by working at many things. His ambition as a young man was to become a pharmacist. While he was working as an apprentice, the Louisiana legislature passed a law requiring a college degree for that profession. Having no money for school, he convinced a friend in Luling to teach him the skills to become a barber. So, he worked in his barber shop, at Shell Oil, and at "making" a garden.

Later in my dad's life he owned a bar and dance hall called the Busy Bee. The bar brought the community together for socializing and dancing. The building that housed the bar later became a laundromat, then an apartment building, and it ended up being the production plant for Mam Papaul products. At the time my father was operating the bar, he was so busy that he could not cut our grass, so he bought two sheep to do the work. They later provided us with two warm, wooly blankets and meat for the table.

Beef at our house came from butchering a family cow or from the traveling "meat man." My mama loved tripe and tongue, and she bought those innard pieces occasionally from a neighbor who worked for a butcher in Luling.

My dad was not a carpenter of any sort, but he did manage to knock together chicken coops and rabbit cages. We always had chickens and a chicken house. Occasionally, when I crossed the yard to go to my grandmother's house, a rooster would get out and chase me. When that happened, my mom made sure he became part of the next Sunday's gumbo pot. Sometimes domestic ducks and a goose or two wound up in the chicken yard, but we did not make pets of them. They, like the chickens and the aggressive roosters, would become Sunday dinner. Mom always said that duck eggs made particularly good cakes.

When I joined the 4-H club in high school, I raised Vantress Cross chickens. That was not a new experience, since I had been feeding, vaccinating, and cleaning chickens since I was a little kid. When it came time to slaughter one, my dad cut the chicken's neck, and it flopped around the yard for a while and wound up in a pot of hot water before my mother and I feathered it. It was not a pleasant experience. Consequently, even though I raised chickens in high school, I did not eat those or any other chickens for a long time.

I suppose you could say my chickens were free range, since they roamed the backyard, where they pecked around in the grass and ate bugs. I also fed them feed corn. They had commercial chicken feed too, but this was long before anyone thought of enhancing chicken food with hormones and antibiotics.

From the beginning, the folks on the German Coast were cooking and eating the wild things they caught, trapped, and shot. That included rabbits, alligators, fresh- and saltwater fish, a variety of birds, crawfish, rabbits, and squirrels. Although my father did own a nice handmade macramé hunting bag, a rifle, and a shotgun, he did not hunt. We had rabbit and squirrel on the dinner table occasionally, but Daddy bought them, mostly from a friend called "Macachew." Seems everyone on the German Coast had a nickname.

Mam Papaul (*left*) has just handed a chicken to her sister Tante Sedonne in the backyard.

Liver and Onions

Makes 4 servings

I was encouraged to eat this dish all my young life because "it's good for you." As an adult, I often ate it when I went out for lunch with my mama. I have to admit, I haven't cooked liver and onions in the last forty years. The last time I made it, I dropped the dish on the floor. I figured that was an omen from the Lord that I should never cook liver and onions again, and I never did. But liver and onions was one of my mother's and grandmother's favorite dishes, and it's still popular in homes all over the German Coast.

1 pound calf liver
1 teaspoon salt, divided
¼ teaspoon cayenne pepper
½ cup all-purpose flour

3 slices bacon
½ stick unsalted butter
1 large onion, chopped
½ cup water

1. Wash liver pieces and pat dry. Check for "tubes" and remove with a sharp-pointed knife. Season with ¾ teaspoon salt and cayenne pepper and dredge in flour. Set aside.
2. In a large skillet set over medium heat, cook bacon to render fat. Remove bacon and set aside.
3. Melt butter with bacon grease in same skillet. Add liver, being careful not to crowd pan, and brown for 2 minutes per side. Remove from pan and set aside.
4. Add onions and remaining ¼ teaspoon salt and cook, stirring occasionally, until caramelized, about 10 minutes. Stir in water and add liver and bacon. Cover and cook until liver is tender and cooked to 160°F, about 15 minutes. Serve warm topped with onion gravy.

The colorful and fragrant sweet peas
Daddy planted for Mom each autumn were fertilized
with droppings from the chicken yard.

Beef Pot Roast with Brown Gravy

Makes 8 servings

Our corner grocery store did not sell fresh meat. Instead, we bought it from the "meat man," who made a weekly pass in his truck on River Road. This roast was served with rice or mashed potatoes and accompanied by buttered *petit pois* (very tiny green peas). Leftovers were used to make poor boy sandwiches.

4-pound chuck or rump roast or
venison tenderloin
3 teaspoons salt
½ teaspoon black pepper
½ teaspoon cayenne pepper
6 cloves garlic, mashed

2 tablespoons oil
½ cup chopped onion
1¼ cups water, divided
2 tablespoons cornstarch
Hot cooked rice for serving

1. Rinse roast and dry with paper towels. Season outside with salt, black pepper, and cayenne pepper. Using a long, sharp knife, make deep cuts into the roast and stuff garlic into slits.
2. Heat oil in a 5-quart Dutch oven set over medium-high heat. Brown roast well. Add onion and ¼ cup water. Cover and cook on low heat until meat is very tender, approximately 2½ hours.
3. Remove meat from pot and stir ½ cup water into pan drippings, scraping the bottom to dissolve brown bits. Skim off excess fat. Mix remaining ½ cup water with cornstarch and stir into pan drippings. Cook on low heat 3 minutes, stirring constantly, to make gravy. Adjust seasonings to taste. Serve gravy over slices of meat and on hot rice.

Beef Pot Roast with Garden Vegetables

Makes 8 servings

Make recipe above, and when the roast is nearly tender, add about 4 cups vegetables such as small potatoes and large chunks of carrot, onion, and turnip. Stir in ½ cup water. Vegetables will cook in the gravy in about 20 minutes and should be served on a platter alongside the roast. We liked this dish, too, served with rice.

Poor Boy Sandwiches

Makes 4 sandwiches

4 (6-inch) pieces fresh French bread
1 pound cooked and sliced beef roast
Leftover gravy
Mayonnaise

Yellow mustard
1 tomato, sliced
4 leaves lettuce, shredded
Sliced dill pickles

1. Heat bread in a preheated 350°F oven until crust is crispy but center is soft, about 5 minutes. Split bread lengthwise.
2. In a saucepan, add meat and gravy and cook over medium heat until bubbly and meat is thoroughly heated, adding water if gravy gets too thick.
3. Spread mayonnaise and mustard on inside of one piece of bread. Pile on beef. Top with gravy, slices of tomato, lettuce, and pickles. Top with second piece of bread. Serve hot. Delicious with cold root beer.

Smothered Ground Beef Sandwiches

Makes 6 sandwiches

This recipe is for whole sandwiches, but Mom served the beef in this recipe folded inside a single slice of soft white bread. That small sandwich, along with a salad and fruit, was a favorite "supper in a hurry." Our last meal of the day was called supper, not dinner. Dinner was the meal served at noon, but we did call it lunch at school.

1 pound ground beef
½ cup finely chopped onion
½ bell pepper, finely chopped

1 teaspoon salt
¼ teaspoon ground black pepper
12 slices white bread

1. In a heavy skillet over medium-high heat, cook ground beef until well browned. Add onion, bell pepper, salt, and pepper, and cook on medium heat until onion is translucent.
2. Divide hot beef mixture among 6 bread slices. Top with anything your heart desires, and cover with remaining slices of bread.

Beef-Stuffed Bell Peppers

Makes 8 servings

Stuffed bell peppers were a popular dish along the river because bell peppers were easy to grow. Many people raised cattle, and shrimp were plentiful from the Mississippi River or nearby Lac des Allemands, so beef and shrimp were often used to stuff bell peppers.

4 large bell peppers
1 pound ground chuck, shrimp, or a
    combination of beef and shrimp
1 cup chopped onion
¾ cup chopped celery
½ cup finely chopped bell pepper

5 cloves garlic, mashed
1 teaspoon salt
½ teaspoon ground black pepper
3 tablespoons unsalted butter
1 cup plain bread crumbs

1. Preheat oven to 350°F. Cut bell peppers in half, from top to bottom, and remove seeds. Cook in a large pot of boiling water until tender, about 5 minutes. Remove and drain.
2. Brown meat over medium-high heat in a large saucepan, or cook shrimp in 3 tablespoons butter until pink. Add onion, celery, chopped bell pepper, garlic, salt, and pepper. Blend well and cook on low heat until vegetables are tender, approximately 15 minutes. Fill pepper halves with stuffing mixture.
3. Melt butter in a small skillet set over medium heat. Add bread crumbs and toast lightly. Top each bell pepper half with bread crumbs. Bake until peppers are tender and tops are deep brown, about 25 minutes.

Daube

Makes 6 servings

This dish is named after the tough French-style roast that old-time cooks in New Orleans simmered until it fell apart. The steaks my mother served were either tough shoulder steaks, round steaks, or seven steaks, which had to go through long, moist-heat cooking. The butcher who came around each week never had anything called a T-bone or sirloin. When I was in high school and the giant Schwegmann's Grocery Store opened twenty miles away, and when we finally had cars and freezers, many families made monthly trips to stock up on groceries. That's when I learned there are other cuts of steak besides seven or round steak.

2 pounds seven steaks or round
  steak
2 teaspoons salt
½ teaspoon ground black pepper, or
  ¼ teaspoon cayenne pepper

4 tablespoons vegetable oil
1 cup chopped onion
2 cups water, divided
2 tablespoons cornstarch
Hot cooked rice for serving

1. Season steaks with salt and pepper. Add oil to a skillet set over medium heat. Brown steak well on both sides.
2. Add onion. Cook until onion is translucent. Add 1½ cups water, cover, and cook on low heat until meat is tender, 30–45 minutes, adding more water if necessary, so there will be enough liquid to make a gravy.
3. Remove meat and keep warm. Mix cornstarch with remaining ½ cup water. Add to skillet, stirring constantly to deglaze pan. Cook over low heat until thickened and season to taste. Pour gravy over meat and serve over hot rice.

Dirty Rice

Makes 6–8 servings

We always called this dish "stuffing," whether it was stuffed in anything or not. Dirty rice was never a main dish, and it's never served in a soup bowl, as is done at local festivals. It was most often used as an accompaniment to fried chicken or to stuff a hen or holiday turkey. In the southwestern part of Louisiana, this dish is called "rice dressing." When I manufactured a product called "rice dressing," it did not sell well. When I changed the name to "dirty rice," it became a best seller.

1 pound bulk breakfast sausage or ground beef
¾ cup chopped onion
¾ cup chopped celery
2 cups water
1 cup raw long-grain white rice
¼ cup chopped green onions
¼ cup chopped parsley
1 teaspoon salt
¼ teaspoon ground black pepper
1 small sweet potato, peeled and grated

1. Place a heavy iron pot over medium heat and brown sausage well. Add onion and celery and turn heat to low. Cook, stirring occasionally, until onions are soft, approximately 8 minutes.
2. Add remaining ingredients and bring to a boil. Cover and turn heat to very low. Cook until rice is soft, about 20 minutes. When rice is cooked, remove from heat and let sit, covered, 10 minutes. Serve hot as a side dish.

Converted Rice or Barley Jambalaya
Makes 12 servings

Most local food historians believe that the Spanish invented jambalaya. John Mariani's *Dictionary of American Food and Drink*, however, says that this one-pot meal was first made to satisfy the hunger of a late-arriving guest at a restaurant in a New Orleans hotel. Not having much in the way of provisions, the cook used leftovers from the noon meal, and he created jambalaya. Converted (parboiled) rice makes a dish with great texture, with grains that are separate. If you're cooking for a crowd and must hold the dish several hours, make your jambalaya with converted rice; it won't get sticky. For a more nutritious jambalaya, substitute barley.

3 slices bacon, diced
4 tablespoons butter, divided
½ cup chopped onion
½ cup chopped celery, with leaves
¼ cup chopped green bell pepper
3 cloves garlic, minced
6 cups water or meat broth
3 cups raw rice or barley
1 pound cooked chicken or turkey

¾ pound diced ham or smoked
    sausage
½ pound shrimp, peeled and
    deveined
½ cup tomato sauce
2 teaspoons Worcestershire sauce
1 teaspoon salt
½ teaspoon ground black pepper
¼ cup chopped parsley

1. Cook bacon until crisp over medium heat in a large skillet. Remove bacon and set aside.
2. Add 2 tablespoons butter to skillet. Sauté onion, celery, bell pepper, and garlic 10 minutes, stirring constantly. Add water. Bring to a boil. Add remaining ingredients, except parsley. Stir well. Cover and cook until rice is tender, about 20–30 minutes.
3. Stir in parsley. Cook an additional 5 minutes. Adjust seasoning to taste and serve warm.

Beef and Potato Hash

Makes 4 servings

When Mama made vegetable soup, she often reserved some of the meat to make hash to serve alongside the soup. I like hash served with freshly sliced apple.

2 tablespoons olive oil
4 medium potatoes, peeled and
    cubed

1 onion, sliced
½ pound cooked and shredded beef
Salt and pepper to taste

1. In a large pot set over medium-high heat, heat oil and cook potatoes until slightly tender and browned. Lower heat to medium. Add onion and cook, stirring often, until caramelized, about 10 minutes Add beef and cook 15 minutes, stirring constantly.
2. By this time, potatoes should be tender. If not, continue cooking. Season with salt and pepper. Serve hot alongside soup.

My mother and father, Lelia and Urbin Tregre,
on the front porch of Mam Papaul's house.

Kidney Stew

Makes 4 servings

This was a dish Mama made for my dad only; for some reason, she never expected us children to eat it. Several years ago, on a trip to London, my husband ordered stewed kidney and enjoyed it. Our daughter Charlena did too, until she found out what she was eating.

1 pound beef or pork kidneys
1½ teaspoons salt, divided
2 teaspoons vinegar or lemon juice
Water
½ cup all-purpose flour, divided
3 strips bacon, in ½-inch slices

4 tablespoons finely chopped onion
2 tablespoons butter
1 tablespoon finely chopped parsley
Mashed potatoes, rice, or toast for
    serving

1. Wash kidneys and remove membrane cover. Cut kidneys in half and remove white fatty cores and tubes.
2. Place kidneys in a 3-quart bowl and add ½ teaspoon salt, vinegar, and 2 cups cold water. Let soak for ½ hour. Drain and rinse in cold water.
3. Cut kidneys into bite-sized pieces and place in a 5-quart pot. Add 2 cups boiling water, cover, and simmer over low heat until tender, about 30 minutes. Drain kidneys and discard liquid.
4. Dredge kidneys in flour and set aside. Reserve remaining flour. Render bacon in a skillet over medium heat. Remove bacon from skillet, leaving fat. Add kidneys and fry until lightly browned. Add onion and cook 5 minutes.
5. Add butter and remaining flour. Stir well for 2 minutes. Deglaze pan with ½ cup water. Add bacon, remaining teaspoon salt, and 2 cups water. Stirring constantly, bring to a boil. Cook until gravy thickens. Adjust seasoning and stir in parsley. Serve over mashed potatoes, rice, or toast.

Chili and Spaghetti
Makes 6–8 servings

At our house, we didn't make chili with beans, and it was not served as a soup. We ladled chili over spaghetti and topped it with grated "stinky" cheese, as we called Parmesan. I guess that's why I was an adult before I realized chili was not an Italian dish. My godfather bought Parmesan cheese from an Italian friend in Waggaman, a small town fifteen miles down River Road on the way to New Orleans. During Lent, Mama sometimes made this red gravy without chili powder and cumin, and she'd poach eggs in it to make a meatless meal. Whenever we had leftover spaghetti, we'd mix it with butter and sugar and make a dish like Jewish noodle kugel.

1 pound ground chuck
1 cup finely chopped onion
½ cup chopped celery
1 (28-ounce) can tomato sauce
1 (28-ounce) can water
1 tablespoon chili powder
1 teaspoon salt

½ teaspoon cumin
¼ teaspoon black pepper or cayenne pepper
1 pound spaghetti, cooked per package directions
Freshly grated Parmesan cheese for serving

1. In a large skillet set over medium heat, cook ground chuck until well browned. Add onion and celery and cook until onions are translucent, about 8 minutes.
2. Add tomato sauce, water, chili powder, salt, cumin, and pepper. Bring to a boil, lower heat, and simmer, stirring occasionally, until gravy thickens, about 30 minutes.
3. Serve chili hot over spaghetti. Top with Parmesan cheese.

Meat or Shrimp Balls in Brown Gravy

Makes 4–6 servings

We like meatballs made with ground beef. Mama tried mixing beef with pork, but that was not for us; she only made them that way once. One of my favorite ways to eat meatballs is in a brown gravy made from pan drippings and served with rice or mashed potatoes. Sometimes we made this dish with shrimp. When made with shrimp, they're called shrimp boulettes.

You've probably noticed by now that we ate a lot of our gravies over rice. Mama, like most others in the community, cooked rice every day. She even had a special pot we called the rice pot. It was a small heavy pot with a tight-fitting lid and was not electric, which is what most Louisiana home cooks use today.

1 pound ground chuck, or 1 pound
   ground shrimp
1¼ cups water, divided
½ cup freshly made bread crumbs
¼ cup finely chopped onion
1 large clove garlic, finely chopped
1 tablespoon finely chopped parsley

1 teaspoon salt
¼ teaspoon black pepper
4 tablespoons vegetable oil
1 tablespoon cornstarch
Hot cooked rice or mashed potatoes
   for serving

1. In a large mixing bowl, combine ground chuck, ½ cup water, bread crumbs, onion, garlic, parsley, salt, and pepper. Make 8 (2-ounce) meatballs.
2. Heat oil over medium heat in a heavy skillet. Brown meatballs on all sides, or place skillet in a 350F° oven and cook until meatballs are well browned. Remove meatballs from skillet and set aside. Continue cooking until fond, a browned crust, has formed on the bottom of the skillet.
3. Deglaze bottom of skillet with ½ cup water. Bring to a simmer. Stir cornstarch into remaining ¼ cup of water. Stir into skillet and cook until gravy is thickened. Add meatballs. Cover and simmer 20 minutes. Season to taste. Serve hot over rice or mashed potatoes.

Chicken Feet

Makes 6 servings

I loved when Mom baked fresh chickens for Sunday dinner because I knew she would roast the chicken's feet along with the chicken. Chicken feet are mostly skin and bones. When cooked, the texture is soft and gelatinous. I adored chicken feet so much that when I found out my favorite children's author, Tomie dePaola, wrote *Watch Out for the Chicken Feet in Your Soup*, I became determined to meet him. I did, and I got him to autograph his collection of fairy tales. My husband bought me an original illustration from the book.

6 chicken feet   Salt and pepper

1. Wash chicken feet well. Remove yellow skin by peeling it off. Chop off toenails. Wash again.
2. Season feet with salt and pepper. Roast with hen as in the following recipe, or separately, wrapped in foil for about 1 hour at 350°F.

Roaſt Chicken

Makes 6–8 servings

With hens pecking in the backyard, you would think chicken was a frequent dish for dinner. That was not the case. Chickens laid eggs we used in other dishes. If we ate the chickens before they stopped laying, we would not have eggs. Chicken was saved for Sunday dinner. For a baked chicken dinner, the star attraction was often a hen that was cooked a long time at a low temperature.

1 (3½–4-pound) chicken   1 cup chicken broth or water,
½ cup (1 stick) unsalted butter   divided
1½ teaspoons salt   1 tablespoon cornstarch
½ teaspoon ground black pepper   Mashed potatoes for serving
¼ cup oil

1. Preheat oven to 350°F. Wash chicken in cold water. Pat dry. Cut into serving-sized pieces.
2. Melt butter and stir in salt and pepper. Rub onto chicken and under skin.
3. Heat oil in a Dutch oven or heavy skillet over medium heat. Brown chicken

pieces well on all sides. Place Dutch oven in oven and bake until internal temperature in thighs reaches 165°F. Allow 15 minutes per pound at 350°F for a hen and 45–60 minutes total for a fryer.

4. Remove chicken and set aside. Deglaze pan with ½ cup broth. Mix cornstarch with remaining ½ cup broth and stir in to make gravy. Cook on low heat until gravy thickens. Season to taste. Serve chicken and gravy with mashed potatoes.

Whole Stuffed Chicken

Makes 6–8 servings

My mom loved to stuff chickens for Sunday dinners, and I loved to help. Although she did not debone her chicken, I do. This recipe taught me the basics of learning to stuff a turkey, which later led to my enthusiasm for learning to do a boneless stuffed turkey, then to make turducken. Bone in or out, this is an impressive presentation. Would Julia Child have approved? Her *French Chef Cookbook* uses many of the same techniques that we use here on the German Coast.

1 (3–4-pound) fryer	½ cup chopped green onions
2 teaspoons salt, divided	¼ cup chopped bell pepper
½ teaspoon ground black pepper	1 cup raw long-grain white rice
¼ teaspoon cayenne pepper	2 cups water
1 pound freshly ground pork or beef	¼ cup chopped parsley
1 cup finely chopped onions	1 apple, halved, core removed
1 cup finely chopped celery	

1. Wash fryer and pat dry with paper towels. Season with 1 teaspoon salt, black pepper, and cayenne pepper. Set aside.
2. Brown ground pork well in a 5-quart pot set over medium-high heat. Add onion, celery, green onions, and bell pepper. Cook until onion is tender and translucent, about 10 minutes. Add rice, water, and remaining teaspoon salt. Bring to a boil. Lower heat, cover, and cook until rice is tender, approximately 20 minutes. Fluff mixture with a fork and stir in parsley. Transfer to a shallow dish and allow to cool.
3. Preheat oven to 375F°. Place chicken in a baking dish and stuff the cavity with cooled dressing. Place half apple in each end of the cavity. If necessary, stitch ends closed with dental floss. Bake until chicken is nicely browned and internal temperature of large pieces reaches 165F°, about 1 hour. Serve hot with any extra stuffing on the side.

Lelia's Fried Chicken

Makes 4–6 servings

Although it seems we always had chickens in the backyard, I do remember a time when my mom and dad would drive to Jefferson, which is close to New Orleans, to buy chickens from merchants who displayed them in wire cages on the sidewalk in front of their stores. Customers chose the chickens they wanted, and the store owner dressed the birds and wrapped them in newspaper for the trip home.

Who can eat just one piece of fried chicken? The preparation concerns that surround frying chicken are tenderness, juiciness, crispiness, and overcooking. My mom could make it all work, but she didn't fry chicken often. I think that was because, when she did, we could never get enough of it. This recipe is based on what I remember as hers. Rabbit is also good prepared this way. My dad raised rabbits for our dinner table, and I am sure we sometimes unknowingly ate rabbit, thinking it was chicken.

1 (3-pound) pound fryer

3 teaspoons salt, divided

2 teaspoons sugar

Vegetable oil or lard for frying

1 large egg

1 cup evaporated milk

1 cup water

2 cups all-purpose flour

½ cup cornstarch

1 teaspoon ground black pepper

¼ teaspoon cayenne pepper

1. Wash fryer and trim off fat. Reserve liver, heart, and gizzard for other uses. Cut chicken into serving-sized pieces. Debone and filet breast if it is very large.
2. Place chicken pieces in a large bowl. Add 2 teaspoons salt and sugar. Fill bowl with water and stir to dissolve salt and sugar. Place in refrigerator 40 minutes. Remove chicken pieces and discard water. Rinse chicken with cool water and pat dry.
3. Add 1½ inches oil to a large skillet or fryer and heat to 350°F. While oil is heating, in a medium bowl, whisk together egg, milk, and 1 cup water. In a gallon-sized, food-safe plastic bag, toss in flour, cornstarch, remaining teaspoon salt, black pepper, and cayenne pepper. Shake well. Dip chicken pieces in egg mixture, allowing excess to drip off. Place a few pieces in the bag of seasoned flour at a time and shake well.
4. Fry a few pieces at a time. Temperature will drop when chicken is added to oil, so try to maintain temperature between 300°F and 325°F. Fry breasts

10–12 minutes, and a little longer for thighs and drumsticks. I like to fry chicken to a 200°F internal temperature. Chicken will be thoroughly cooked and still be tasty and juicy. Place cooked chicken on a rack (not on paper towels) and keep warm in the oven.

German Coast Chicken Stew

Makes 8 servings

My dad loved chicken stew with mushrooms—you know, those little rubbery things from the can. That is what my mama used. Our grocery stores didn't carry fresh mushrooms back then, and no way did my dad trust himself to pick wild mushrooms for us to eat. I do, however, have an uncle whose mother made wild mushroom stew with mushrooms picked from a field behind their family home in Edgard.

1 (4-pound) hen
Salt and pepper
½ cup vegetable oil
½ cup all-purpose flour
¾ cup chopped onion
½ cup chopped celery
2 quarts hot chicken broth or
    water

1 (5-ounce) can button mushrooms,
    or 5 ounces small, fresh button
    mushrooms
2 tablespoons chopped green onions
2 tablespoons chopped parsley
Salt and pepper to taste
Hot cooked rice or mashed potatoes
    for serving

1. Preheat oven to 350°F. Cut hen into serving pieces and season generously with salt and pepper. Place in a Dutch oven and bake, uncovered, until chicken turns brown, about 20 minutes. Remove chicken from pot and set aside.
2. Add oil and flour to pot and cook over medium heat, stirring constantly, to make a roux the color of a dark penny. Add onions and celery and cook 10 minutes over low heat, stirring constantly.
3. Add chicken and broth and stir. Cover and simmer until chicken is tender and gravy is free of lumps. (Since this is a hen, it might take two hours or more to tenderize.) Add additional water if necessary.
4. Add mushrooms, green onions, and parsley. Add salt and pepper to taste. Continue cooking 10 minutes. Gravy should be thick. Serve with rice or mashed potatoes.

Chicken or Alligator Sauce Piquante

Makes 6–8 servings

Sauce piquante is historically a dish men prepared for male friends after a hunting or fishing trip. The stewlike dish is often made at local bars and hunting camps with whatever was hunted that day, such as venison, rabbit, turtle, alligator, or squirrel. There is a local controversy over whether the sauce should be a red gravy, a brown gravy, or a combination of the two. No controversy exists over the heat level; the hotter the better, according to most. Chicken sauce piquante is a home version of what was usually made away from home with game.

1 (5-pound) chicken, or 5 pounds alligator meat
1 tablespoon salt
1 teaspoon ground black pepper
½ cup vegetable oil or rendered chicken fat
½ cup all-purpose flour
2½ cups chopped onion
1½ cups chopped celery
¾ cup chopped green bell pepper
4 teaspoons finely chopped garlic
2 (8-ounce) cans tomato sauce

1 (1-pound, 1-ounce) can whole tomatoes, with liquid
2 cups hot water or chicken broth
2 bay leaves
2 (6-ounce) cans mushrooms or 2 cups sliced fresh mushrooms
½ cup chopped green onions
½ cup chopped parsley
1 tablespoon Tabasco or your favorite hot sauce
Hot cooked rice for serving

1. Cut chicken into serving pieces and season with salt and pepper. Heat oil in a large skillet set over medium-high heat and brown chicken well on all sides. Set aside.
2. Add flour to oil remaining in skillet and cook, stirring constantly, to make a light-brown roux. Add onion, celery, bell pepper, and garlic. Continue cooking 10 minutes, stirring constantly.
3. Add chicken pieces, tomato sauce, tomatoes and liquid, hot water, and bay leaves. Cover and cook on low heat until chicken is tender. (A hen will be tender in about 2 hours, a fryer in about 45 minutes.) Remove bay leaves.
4. Add mushrooms, green onions, parsley, and Tabasco sauce. Continue cooking 10 minutes. Serve chicken and sauce hot over rice.

Chicken Pot Pie

Makes 8 servings

Mama's first attempts at chicken pot pie featured a brown gravy much like the roux-based kind she made for chicken stew. Since we liked her white sauce served over boiled vegetables, it wasn't a stretch for us to learn to love this version of chicken pot pie, one that she and I first made together. Use fresh mushrooms in this recipe, but not fresh from the forest behind your house unless you're sure they're not poisonous.

1 (4–5-pound) chicken
1 carrot, quartered
½ cup chopped onion
½ cup chopped celery
2 tablespoons chopped parsley
1 teaspoon salt
½ teaspoon ground black pepper
2 store-bought refrigerated pie crusts
8 tablespoons unsalted butter, divided

4 tablespoons all-purpose flour
2 cups chicken broth (from boiling chicken)
1 pound mushrooms, sliced
⅓ cup heavy cream
2 tablespoons diced pimento
2 tablespoons chopped bell pepper
Salt and pepper to taste
1 large egg
2 tablespoons water

1. Place chicken, carrot, onion, celery, and parsley in a large boiling pot. Add salt and pepper. Cover chicken with water. Bring water to a boil and simmer until chicken is tender. (A fryer will be boiled tender in 45 minutes.) Remove chicken, reserving broth.
2. When chicken is cool enough to handle, remove meat from bones and discard bones and skin. Cut meat into chunks and set aside. Boil broth vigorously and reduce to 2 cups. Strain and set aside.
3. Place one pie crust in a deep pie dish, preferably clear (so you will be able to check the browning of the lower crust). Place in refrigerator until ready to use. Preheat oven to 400°F.
4. Melt 3 tablespoons butter in a small skillet. Add flour and stir well. Whisk in reserved broth. Cook until sauce thickens.
5. Sauté mushrooms in remaining 5 tablespoons butter until soft. Add mushrooms to sauce along with chicken, cream, pimento, and bell pepper. Season to taste with salt and pepper. Place creamed mixture in pie shell. Top with second pastry and crimp edges. Beat egg with 2 tablespoons water and brush top crust with egg wash. Make two 2-inch slits in top of pie. Bake until top and bottom of pie is lightly browned and bubbles appear through the slits, about 50 minutes. Serve warm.

Chicken and Spaghetti

Makes 8 servings

This was a dish that showed up often at church fairs and was popular for Sunday dinners. Say "chicken and spaghetti" on the German Coast, and we think "red gravy." In other parts of Louisiana, it would be a cream gravy, according to my husband's relatives from Leesville. Since I raised chickens for 4-H contests, they have a special place in my heart. One year it rained right before a show, and my beautiful white Vantress Cross chickens got muddy. I couldn't show dirty chickens, so I shampooed their feathers and dried them with my hair dryer. They took second place.

1 (3-pound) chicken (a fryer will
    cook faster than a hen)
2½ teaspoons salt
¼ teaspoon ground black pepper
¼ teaspoon cayenne pepper
¼ cup olive oil
2 cups chopped onion
1 cup chopped celery

2 cloves garlic, chopped
1 (4-ounce) can tomato sauce
1 large can whole tomatoes, with
    juice
1½ quarts water
1 (10-ounce) package spaghetti,
    cooked per package directions

1. Preheat oven to 375°F. Cut chicken into serving pieces and season with salt, black pepper, and cayenne pepper. Bake until chicken has browned, about 25 minutes.
2. Heat oil in a 5-quart pot set over medium-high heat. Add onion, celery, and garlic. Cook, stirring constantly, until vegetables are golden, about 15 minutes.
3. Add chicken with pan juices, tomato sauce, whole tomatoes and juice, and water. Bring to a boil. Reduce heat, cover, and simmer until chicken is tender and sauce has thickened, about 40 minutes. Adjust seasoning to taste. Serve hot over spaghetti.

Chicken Salad for a Crowd

Makes 9 cups, enough for 18 whole sandwiches

Anytime there is a baby shower, wedding, or celebration of any kind on the German Coast, chicken salad sandwiches are on the menu. My aunt Adeline was the go-to person for big batches of chicken salad. She used homemade mayonnaise made with two hard-boiled egg yolks. Mom used fresh whole eggs in her mayonnaise. It was fascinating to watch her add the oil in, drop by drop. This recipe also makes a great dip.

Boiled Chicken

1 (6-pound) baking hen or large fryer
3 teaspoons salt
1 medium onion, unpeeled and
  quartered
2 ribs celery, chopped
2 small carrots

Place chicken in a large soup pot and cover with water. Add remaining ingredients and bring to a boil. Lower heat and cook chicken until tender, about 1 hour. Place on a platter to cool, reserving stock for another use. Remove skin and debone. Coarsely chop chicken.

Chicken Salad

6–7 cups chopped chicken (meat
  from the boiled 6-pound chicken)
6 hard-boiled eggs, chopped
¾ cup chopped dill pickle
¾ cup chopped pimento-stuffed
  olives
½ cup finely chopped celery
2½–3 cups mayonnaise, commercial
  or homemade (recipe page 104)
½ teaspoon prepared yellow mustard
1½ teaspoons Creole seasoning for
  seafood (I use K-Paul's Seafood
  Magic.) (optional)

Place all ingredients in a large bowl. Mix well. Make sandwiches or serve with crackers.

Stuffed Turkey, with Extra Turkey Necks
Makes 10–12 servings

No smell makes me want to jump out of bed faster than the aroma of a roasting turkey. On holidays, we children all begged for a taste of turkey before it hit the dining table. To stop our pleading, Mama would snitch the neck from the roasting pan and let us share it. That was a special treat. Now when I bake turkey, I throw in extra necks.

These days, I brine my turkeys. Brining is not a technique traditional to our area, but the result makes such a dramatically moist turkey, I thought I'd include that step in this recipe.

1 (10–12-pound) turkey
3 turkey necks
½ cup, plus 1 tablespoon salt
⅓ cup sugar
1 teaspoon black pepper
1 teaspoon garlic powder or 6 cloves
    garlic, chopped
1 stick unsalted butter, melted

1 teaspoon powdered sage (optional)
⅔ cup dry vermouth
1 recipe cooled Turkey Stuffing
    (recipe follows)
1 apple, halved, core removed
1½ cups unsalted chicken broth or
    water, divided
4 tablespoons cornstarch

1. Wash turkey and necks in cool water. Remove innards and reserve for stuffing.
2. Place turkey in a large, clean, food-safe plastic or nonreactive metal container with ½ cup salt and sugar. Add enough water to cover the bird. Place in refrigerator at least 2 hours or overnight. Drain and dry turkey.
3. In a small bowl, mix together remaining tablespoon salt, pepper, garlic powder, butter, sage, and vermouth. Pull skin away from turkey meat section by section. Pierce meat, not skin, with a fork at 2-inch intervals. Rub seasoning under skin and in cavity. Refrigerate turkey 2 hours.
4. Remove turkey from refrigerator and stuff with Turkey Stuffing (recipe below). Push half apple into each end of turkey cavity. Close each opening with a skewer or sew with heavy thread or dental floss.
5. Preheat oven to 325°F. Place turkey, breast side up, on rack in a roaster. Place necks in the bottom of the pan. Cover and bake until temperature in thigh and center of stuffing reaches 170°F, about 2½ hours or 15 minutes per pound. Remove from oven and tent with foil 20 minutes.
6. Meanwhile, make gravy by draining drippings from roasting pan. Place roaster back in oven to allow fond, a brown crust, to form on the bottom

of the pan. Add ½ cup broth to roasting pan and stir over medium-high heat to remove brown bits. Mix remaining cup of broth with cornstarch and whisk into broth in roasting pan to make a gravy. Simmer 10 minutes, stirring constantly.

7. Remove turkey to a carving board. Slice, cutting across the grain on the breast, and arrange pieces on a platter. Serve turkey warm along with gravy.

Turkey Stuffing

Makes enough to stuff a 10–12-pound turkey

2 pounds ground pork
Liver, gizzard, and heart from
    turkey, all ground or finely
    chopped
2 cups chopped onion
1½ cups chopped celery
½ cup chopped bell pepper
6 cloves garlic, mashed

½ cup chopped parsley
½ cup chopped green onions
2½ teaspoons salt
½ teaspoon ground black pepper
5 cups water
2½ cups long grain rice
1 sweet potato, grated
1 dozen oysters, shucked (optional)

1. Brown pork and chopped liver, gizzard, and heart over medium heat in a large saucepan. Add onion, celery, bell pepper, garlic, parsley, and green onions. Cook until onion becomes translucent, about 10 minutes.

2. Stir in salt, pepper, water, rice, and sweet potato. Bring water to a boil. Lower heat, cover, and cook for 20 minutes.

3. Stir in oysters. Cook until edges of oysters curl and rice is tender, about 10 more minutes. Cool thoroughly in refrigerator, then stuff into turkey cavity.

Roast Goose

Makes 8–12 servings

Dell Gourgues, who is of German descent and married to my cousin Elmore Gourgues, says her mom often cooked goose. Growing up, the only time we had roast goose was when a lone goose in our backyard ran after my brother, who was riding his new Schwinn bicycle, and the goose somehow got his leg caught in the spokes. We celebrated that Easter with a goose dinner that we still talk about.

Today, when I roast a goose, I often bard (cover) the goose with bacon and stuff it with chunks of raw onion. I also think goose needs an extra dab of pepper. We used cayenne in just about everything we cooked, but our food was not so blistering hot that the children could not enjoy it. Roast goose makes a rich gravy, which balances nicely with dried fruit, such as prunes.

1 (6- to 8-pound) goose	1 cup chopped onion
1½ teaspoons salt	2 cups prunes
½ teaspoon cayenne pepper	2 cups chicken broth, divided
4 cloves garlic, mashed	2 tablespoons cornstarch
½ pound sliced bacon	

1. Preheat oven to 325°F. Wash the goose and pat dry. Season inside and out with salt, pepper, and garlic. Prick goose all over on the inside, being careful not to puncture the skin. Bard (cover) the goose with bacon.
2. Place goose breast side up on a rack in a large roaster. Add onion. Surround goose with prunes, cover, and bake until goose is tender, usually 15 minutes per pound.
3. Remove goose from pan, set aside, and cover with foil to keep warm. Skim off as much fat as possible, or defat in a glass jar or large glass measuring cup. Reserve prunes separately. Add 1 cup broth and defatted drippings to the pan and deglaze over medium-high heat. Stir cornstarch into remaining cup of broth and stir into pan juices. Cook until thickened. Add reserved prunes and bring to a boil. Serve goose warm with gravy and prunes.

Smothered Quail or Doves

Makes 8 servings

My grandfather Papaul loved to hunt quail, and my brother, Euclid, enjoyed hunting doves. This was my mom's favorite way of preparing game birds.

8 large quail, dressed
Salt and pepper

1 pound sliced bacon
8 oysters

1. Preheat oven to 375°F. Season quail with salt and pepper. Wrap a piece of bacon around each oyster. Stuff a bacon-wrapped oyster into each quail cavity. Wrap each quail in bacon and secure with toothpicks.
2. Bake until bacon is brown and crispy, approximately 20 minutes. Serve warm.

A few days before Easter, Mémère Nellie would gather chicken eggs from her henhouse and place wet clover leaves and a variety of grasses flat on the surfaces of the eggs. She wrapped the grass-covered eggs tightly in cheesecloth and tied it with a string. She placed the eggs in a pot of boiling water and onion skins, covered the pot, and turned off the heat. Fifteen minutes later, the eggs came out of the water. Mémère would unwrap the cheesecloth to reveal beautiful rust-colored eggs with leaf designs imprinted onto the shells. She then hid them in the backyard for her great-grandchildren to find.

Blackbird Jambalaya

Makes 6 servings

Even though blackbirds are protected under the Federal Migratory Bird Treaty Act, in Louisiana, they can be hunted when they are harming agricultural crops or when concentrations of them become a nuisance. My mama never indulged my dad with this dish he enjoyed in his childhood, but he did tell us about it. Blackbirds were numerous on my grandfather's little farm in Wallace, thirty-five miles upriver from New Orleans, so I imagine that he did have this dish. Since it's unlikely you have a stash of blackbirds, try making this jambalaya with quail or doves.

6 small game birds, feathered and gutted
2 teaspoons salt
½ teaspoon cayenne pepper
4 slices bacon
½ cup water
⅓ cup chopped onion
2 cups chicken broth or water
½ cup chopped bell pepper
½ cup chopped green onions
1 medium tomato, finely chopped
2 tablespoons chopped parsley
1 cup raw rice

1. Season birds with salt and pepper. In a large skillet set over medium heat, render fat from bacon. Remove bacon from pan, leaving drippings.
2. Add birds to pan and brown lightly. Add water, cover, and cook until birds are tender, about 30 minutes for small quail or doves. Remove birds and set aside.
3. Add onions to the skillet and cook to a light brown. Add broth to deglaze pan. Add birds and remaining ingredients. Cover and cook over low heat until rice is tender, approximately 25 minutes. Crumble bacon and add. Stir and serve.

Smothered Rabbit or Squirrel

Makes 4 servings

Most times, while my brother and dad were enjoying this delectable dish, my mom, sister, and I were dining on fried fresh Amedee pork sausage with a serving of Saturday white beans and rice. Mr. Amedee lived across the street, and he owned a grocery store. Our other across-the-street-neighbor was Mr. Po'boy, his wife, Ms. Jonise, and her sisters, Miss Teen and Miss Po. These ladies always greeted us with a friendly "*eh, là-bah.*" In Cajun French that means, "Hey, over there." My mom often visited with these friends, who enjoyed watching the goings-on in the neighborhood from their rockers on the front porch.

They also loved eating Mam Papaul's cakes, which she generously shared with them. I can still remember hearing them graciously thanking her with "Many thanks, many thanks," as we'd step off their porch to go home.

1 domestic or wild rabbit or 1 squirrel, cut into serving pieces	1 cup chopped onion
Milk, enough to cover meat	1 bunch green onions, chopped
Salt and ground black pepper	¼ cup chopped parsley
3 tablespoons oil	¼ cup water

1. Soak rabbit in milk for two hours. Rinse and pat dry. Season with salt and pepper.
2. Place oil in a 4-quart Dutch oven set over medium heat. Brown rabbit well on all sides.
3. Add remaining ingredients and stir well. Add additional water, if necessary. Cover and cook on low heat until rabbit is well done and tender or when internal temperature reaches 165°F. Serve hot.

Pan-Seared Venison Cutlets

Makes 8 servings

Most men on the German Coast owned a shotgun or rifle that they used for hunting squirrel and deer. My Pépère Tregre hunted rabbits, too, and he also trapped them in rabbit boxes. As I've mentioned, my dad did not hunt anything, but many of my uncles, cousins, and friends loved to hunt deer.

6 venison cutlets from a tenderloin, each ½ inch or thicker	1 teaspoon salt
Powdered meat tenderizer	¼ teaspoon cayenne pepper
2 teaspoons ground thyme	6 slices bacon
	2 tablespoons cooking oil

1. Preheat oven to 350°F. Wipe meat dry with a paper towel. Season cutlets with a light sprinkling of tenderizer, thyme, salt, and cayenne pepper.
2. Wrap perimeter of each cutlet with a slice of bacon and secure with a toothpick. Heat oil in skillet until very hot but not smoking. When oil is very hot, place meat in skillet. Sear both sides well. Do not crowd skillet.
3. Place skillet with venison in oven to finish cooking to desired doneness. Tent with foil 6 minutes and serve.

Fried Frog Legs
Makes 2 servings

My mom and brother were the only ones who ate this French specialty. Many men on the German Coast would "bull-eye" in the swamp for frogs. Bull-eying involved wearing a light on your head, which would blind the frogs so they could easily be caught. My dad was not much of a sportsman. Instead, he was the epitome of the stereotypical German; he didn't have much time for fun, nor did he neglect his work to have fun. My brother, on the other hand, liked hanging around with his buddies, and he usually managed to catch a few bullfrogs when he and friends went bull-eyeing.

Vegetable oil for frying
8 hind legs from large bullfrogs
1¾ teaspoons salt, divided
¾ teaspoon ground black pepper, divided
¼ teaspoon cayenne pepper
¾ cup evaporated milk

1 large egg
¼ cup water
1½ cups all-purpose flour
1 teaspoon grated lemon rind
Tartar sauce for serving (recipe page 99)

1. Heat 2 inches oil to 350°F in a deep skillet or fryer. Skin and wash frog legs. Pat dry. Season with 1 teaspoon salt, ½ teaspoon black pepper, and cayenne pepper.
2. In a large, shallow bowl, whisk together milk, egg, and water. In a gallon-sized, food-safe plastic bag, mix together flour, lemon rind, remaining ¾ teaspoon salt, and remaining ¼ teaspoon black pepper. Shake well. Dip frog legs in egg mixture, then place in bag with flour and shake well to coat.
3. Fry a few pieces at a time in hot oil, maintaining oil temperature between 300°F and 325°F. Fry until legs are brown and cooked through, about 8 to 10 minutes. Serve hot with tartar sauce.

SEAFOOD

CÔTE DES ALLEMANDS (Coast of the Germans) is not really a coast in the traditional sense but is on the banks of the Mississippi River. We also have a large lake, Lac (Lake) des Allemands, which is a natural 12,000-acre body of water bordered by the parishes of St. John the Baptist, Lafourche, and St. Charles. Our shallow lake is fed by a maze of bayous, canals, and channels, and it is rich in bass, sac-a-lait, bream, and, especially, catfish. Lac des Allemands is home to so many catfish that in 1975 Governor Edwin Edwards signed a proclamation declaring the adjoining town of Des Allemands the Catfish Capital of the World. In 1980, the Louisiana legislature topped that and passed a resolution proclaiming Des Allemands the Catfish Capital of the Universe.

In the early days, the people of Des Allemands were typically trappers and fishermen. They did not sell their seafood, which was a mainstay of their diet. Over the years, along with selling alligator hides and mink and nutria pelts, they made fishing into a lucrative industry.

My family absolutely loved just about any kind of seafood. My dad was not too fond of fishing, but he made an effort to introduce the sport to my brother, Euclid. Eventually, Euclid's avocation was designing and making fishing lures, and he built up a corporation doing just that. He sold his company, Rhumba Lures, a few years ago.

When we were children, our seafood dinners sometimes centered on the perch my brother caught in a nearby crevasse. And there was always river shrimp from the Mississippi River. One of the best things about river shrimp was that they were free.

Until the 1970s, crawfish was not something anyone bought; everyone caught their own crawfish in the nearby swamps. Sometimes a heavy rain brought swarms of crawfish crawling onto nearby roads, and they were free for the picking by those brave enough to face the traffic. That was not something we were allowed to do.

By the time I got to high school, truck vendors were selling shrimp and crab along the sides of our roads. We were huge fans of crab. Mama usually bought boiled crabs for us to enjoy. Daddy sold boiled crabs on Friday nights at his bar, the Busy Bee. On Sunday afternoons, the Busy Bee turned into a community meeting place, where ladies from the neighborhood listened to the jukebox, bought ice cream, and gossiped. The men enjoyed a beer or two and played pool while the jukebox played the latest tunes. I remember listening to "If I Knew You Were Comin' I'd've Baked a Cake" and "Red Silk Stockings and Green Perfume."

Every member of the family went crawfishing in our swamp.
This is my mother Lelia holding my youngest sister, Briget Cornwell.

Shrimp Remoulade

Makes 2½ cups sauce, enough for 12 servings

Even though remoulade is associated with New Orleans, I learned to make this sauce when I was in college in Lafayette. After I brought this recipe home, Mama made it often, and it became a family favorite. On a hot summer day, there is no better way to enjoy boiled shrimp than when they're bathed with spicy remoulade sauce.

1 cup extra virgin olive oil
½ cup coarsely chopped celery
½ cup chopped green onions
5 tablespoons white or cider vinegar
5 tablespoons catsup
3 tablespoons yellow prepared
   mustard
3 tablespoons prepared horseradish

3 tablespoons freshly squeezed
   lemon juice
2 teaspoons paprika
1½ teaspoons salt
½ teaspoon ground black pepper
¼ teaspoon cayenne pepper
3 pounds large boiled shrimp, peeled
   and deveined
Crackers for serving

1. Place all ingredients except shrimp in a blender. Blend on medium speed 12 minutes.
2. Spoon over cold boiled shrimp. Serve with crackers.

Daddy caught river shrimp in a homemade wooden shrimp box.
Occasionally, we were allowed to help raise the boxes.
But that was considered dangerous because
the water moccasins that slithered along the levee
made my mom fear for our lives.

Barbecued Shrimp

Makes 6–8 servings

During the 1950s, seafood from Lac des Allemands became more available, and we started experimenting with new shrimp recipes. Barbecued shrimp was one of them. The first barbecued shrimp recipe was developed at Pascal's Manale Restaurant in New Orleans. Barbecued shrimp aren't grilled or covered in red barbecue sauce. They're either sautéed or baked, and sometimes both, in a garlicky butter sauce. If you like shrimp, you'll love this dish.

3 pounds large, unpeeled, head-on shrimp (21–25 per pound)
1 cup (2 sticks) unsalted butter
1 cup olive oil
6–8 cloves garlic, mashed
2 tablespoons Worcestershire sauce (optional)

1 tablespoon Louisiana hot sauce or your favorite, to taste
1 tablespoon Italian seasoning, or 1 teaspoon each finely chopped oregano, thyme, and rosemary
1 tablespoon ground black pepper
1½ teaspoons red pepper flakes
Hot French bread for serving

1. Preheat oven to 375°F. Rinse and drain shrimp. Leave shells and heads on. (Some people like to suck the heads after cooking to enjoy the flavorful juices.) Set aside.
2. In a medium saucepan over medium heat, melt butter. Add olive oil, garlic, Worcestershire sauce, hot sauce, Italian seasoning, black pepper, and red pepper flakes. Cook on low heat 10 minutes.
3. Spread shrimp in a large rimmed baking pan and pour on butter mixture. Mix well to coat shrimp.
4. Bake 10 minutes. Stir to turn shrimp. Cook until shrimp have turned pink, an additional 10 minutes. Serve in bowls with crispy, hot French bread on the side to sop up the juices.

Fried Shrimp Balls

Makes 6 servings

5 tablespoons butter, divided
3 tablespoons finely chopped onion
2 tablespoons finely chopped parsley
2 tablespoons finely chopped celery
1 pound shrimp, peeled and deveined
  and finely chopped
2 teaspoons lemon juice
½ teaspoon salt

¼ teaspoon ground black pepper
½ cup flour
½ cup whole milk
¾ cup milk
Vegetable oil for frying
2 cups seasoned bread crumbs
2 tablespoons water
2 large eggs, slightly beaten

1. Melt 2 tablespoons butter in a large skillet over medium heat and sauté onion, parsley, and celery 10 minutes, stirring constantly. Add shrimp and cook until shrimp turn pink. Stir in lemon juice, salt, and pepper. Set aside.
2. In a medium-sized saucepan over medium heat, melt remaining 3 tablespoons butter. Stir in flour. Whisk in milk and bring to a boil. Remove from heat and add shrimp mixture. Mix well.
3. Heat 1½ inches oil in a fryer or deep skillet to 360°F. Shape shrimp mixture into 2-ounce balls and set them aside. Spread bread crumbs in a shallow bowl. In a separate small, shallow bowl, beat water into eggs to make an egg wash. Roll balls in bread crumbs, dip into egg wash, then roll again in bread crumbs. Fry balls in hot oil a few at a time until light golden brown. Serve hot.

*I have a special memory of me and my mama
in the wash shed behind our house. That's where she
kept her stash of preserved foods, which sometimes
included jars of river shrimp cooked in butter.*

Shrimp and Potato Stew

Makes 4–6 servings

Even though this dish contains potatoes, we always enjoyed it served over rice. Yes, we on the German Coast like our starches.

½ cup vegetable oil
½ cup all-purpose flour
¾ cup chopped onion
½ cup chopped celery
5 cups hot water
4 medium red potatoes, peeled and diced

1 pound medium shrimp, peeled and deveined, or crawfish tails
1 (4-ounce) can tomato sauce
⅓ cup chopped bell pepper
1 bay leaf
½ teaspoon salt
¼ teaspoon ground black pepper
Hot cooked rice for serving

1. Heat oil in a heavy skillet set over a medium flame. Add flour and stir constantly to make a dark roux. Should take about 8–10 minutes.
2. Add onion and celery. Cook 10 minutes, stirring constantly. Add water, potatoes, shrimp, tomato sauce, bell pepper, bay leaf, salt, and pepper. Simmer over low heat for 30 minutes. Remove bay leaf. Adjust seasoning to taste. Serve hot over rice.

Traditional Jambalaya with Shrimp and Ham

Makes 8 servings

There are as many recipes for jambalaya as there are families on the German Coast. I grew up eating red jambalaya made with tomato sauce, and I think it is the best. Other jambalaya fans up the river swear by brown jambalaya cooked with lima beans. However, we only argue about jambalaya's color—should it be brown or red? Since this recipe is made with tomato and is similar to what's traditionally cooked in New Orleans, I guess this could be called a Creole jambalaya. I make it with shrimp and ham, but many combinations of meat, poultry, and fish work well, too. Go ahead and experiment with your favorites.

3 tablespoons olive oil	1 teaspoon salt
2 cups raw long-grain rice	1 pound shrimp, peeled and deveined
1 cup chopped onion	½ pound andouille or ham, diced
½ cup chopped green onions	3½ cups water, or chicken or ham
½ cup chopped celery	stock
½ cup chopped bell pepper	4 ounces tomato sauce
3 cloves garlic, chopped	¼ cup chopped parsley

1. In a Dutch oven set over medium-high heat, heat oil and add rice. Stir and fry until rice turns white.
2. Add onion, green onion, celery, bell pepper, garlic, and salt. Cook until onion turns translucent, about 5 minutes.
3. Add shrimp and andouille, water, tomato sauce, and parsley. Bring to a boil. Cover, lower heat to a bare simmer, and cook until rice is tender and all of liquid is absorbed, approximately 30 minutes. Fluff and serve hot.

One of my prized possessions is a very big and heavy
iron pot that my husband bought for me
to cook a big pot of jambalaya.

Shrimp-Stuffed Bell Peppers

Makes 12 servings

This is the best recipe for shrimp-stuffed bell peppers I have ever tried. My friend Elsie, who is from the town of Ama, gave this recipe to her daughter to pass on to me because I raved about it so much at a church fair.

3 large bell peppers, seeded and
  sliced in half lengthwise
3–4 tablespoons butter, divided
1 pound shrimp, peeled and deveined
1 medium tomato, chopped
1½ cups chopped onion

½ cup finely chopped bell pepper
1 tablespoon chopped parsley
1 teaspoon salt
Pinch cayenne pepper
1 cup plain bread crumbs, divided

1. Preheat oven to 350°. Boil bell pepper halves 5 minutes. Drain and set aside.
2. Melt 1 tablespoon butter in a skillet set over low heat and cook shrimp until they turn pink, about 2 minutes. Add tomato, onion, chopped bell pepper, parsley, salt, and cayenne pepper. Mix well. Slowly cook until onion is translucent and bell pepper is tender.
3. Remove from heat and stir in ½ cup bread crumbs. Mixture should be soft and not dry. If it is dry, add another tablespoon of butter, melted.
4. Stuff bell pepper halves with shrimp mixture. Melt remaining 2 tablespoons butter and mix with remaining ½ cup bread crumbs. Top stuffed peppers with bread crumb mixture. Place in a baking pan and bake until heated through and bread crumbs are lightly browned, about 30 minutes. Serve hot.

Crab-Stuffed Shrimp

Makes 4 servings

Oh, shrimp, how do I love thee? We cook shrimp too many ways to try to record them all, but crab-stuffed shrimp is a German Coast favorite.

1 pound crabmeat, lump or claw
16 large raw jumbo shrimp, peeled
and deveined
½ cup (1 stick) butter
½ cup finely chopped celery
½ cup finely chopped onion
½ cup finely chopped green onions
¼ cup finely chopped bell pepper
4 cloves garlic, minced
2 sleeves saltine crackers, finely
crushed, divided

½ teaspoon dried thyme
½ teaspoon salt
¼ teaspoon dried oregano
¼ teaspoon powdered bay leaf
(optional)
¼ teaspoon black pepper or cayenne
pepper to taste
4 large eggs, divided
Vegetable oil for frying
2 tablespoons water
Chopped parsley for garnish

1. Pick through crabmeat and remove shells. Butterfly shrimp by slicing down the back almost, but not quite all the way, through. Rinse and drain shrimp and spread each one open until they are almost flat.
2. Melt butter in a skillet over medium heat. Sauté celery, onion, green onions, bell pepper, and garlic until onion turns translucent, about 5 minutes. Remove from heat. Add half of crushed saltines, thyme, salt, oregano, bay leaf, and pepper. Mix well. Gently stir in crabmeat. Add remaining cracker crumbs to a large, shallow bowl.
3. Whisk two eggs and gently stir into crabmeat mixture. Divide crabmeat mixture into 16 portions.
4. Preheat 1½ inches oil in a fryer or deep pot to 350°F. Place 1 portion of crabmeat on top of each butterflied shrimp. Bring sides of shrimp up around stuffing as much as possible. Beat remaining 2 eggs with water. Dip each stuffed shrimp into egg wash, then into cracker crumbs. Fry in hot oil until lightly browned. Alternately, brush with butter and broil until shrimp turn pink, about 10 minutes, turning once. Garnish with parsley and serve immediately.

Hot Shrimp Étouffée Dip

Makes 3 cups

When I used to participate in food shows, this was one of the quick and easy hot dips I developed to showcase the versatility of Mam Papaul's Creole Étouffée Mix. This creamy dip can also be used as a sauce for pasta.

1 cup small shrimp, peeled and
    deveined
4 tablespoons (½ stick) butter
1 package (2.5 ounces) Mam Papaul's
    Creole Étouffée Mix (from grocery
    specialty stores or purchase online)

1 pint sour cream
Hot sauce, to taste
Crackers or French bread for serving

1. In a skillet set over medium-high heat, sauté shrimp in butter until shrimp turn pink.
2. Add étouffée mix and sour cream. Heat on low 8 minutes, stirring constantly. Season with hot sauce. Serve warm with crackers or French bread. (This is a good dip to use in a chafing dish.)

Mam Papaul's Hot Crawfish Pie Dip

Makes 3 cups

Here is another hot dip I developed, this one to showcase Mam Papaul's Crawfish Pie Mix. As anyone from Louisiana knows, a crawfish pie is filled with a savory blend of spices and crawfish tails. This dip has the traditional crawfish pie flavor and a much creamier texture. At food shows, I could never make enough to last throughout a three-day event. People would bring plates from other booths and request a serving.

1 (12- or 16-ounce) package frozen
    crawfish tails
4 tablespoons (½ stick) butter
1 cup water
1 package (2.75 ounces) Mam Papaul's
    Crawfish Pie Mix (from grocery
    or specialty stores or online)

1 (8-ounce) package cream cheese
A few tablespoons milk or cream
Crackers or pasta for serving

1. Thaw crawfish tails, remove from package, and soak in cold water 10 minutes. Drain and discard liquid.
2. In a large skillet set over medium heat, sauté crawfish tails in butter 5 minutes. Add water and crawfish pie mix. Simmer 8 minutes, stirring constantly.
3. Add cream cheese and stir until melted. Thin to desired consistency with a little milk or cream. Serve warm as a dip with crackers or over pasta as a main dish.

Boiled Crawfish, Crabs, or Shrimp

Makes 6 servings

My grandfather Leopold took special pride in his big, black boiling pot, since they were hard to come by. That iron kettle served the family for winter boucheries, as well as for boiling whatever seafood was in season. Whenever seafood was on the menu, the crabs, crawfish, and shrimp, along with potatoes and corn, were spread on the table and eaten as soon as they were cool enough to handle. There would be plenty of cold beer and soft drinks. Nothing else was served, except maybe crackers. Mama, however, liked buttered white rice with her boiled crawfish. And sometimes hot double-dipped garlic bread also made an accompaniment. If there were leftovers, I'd get to enjoy boiled seafood my favorite way, cold and served with a tomato cocktail sauce.

Water for boiling seafood
1 (3-ounce) bag dry crab boil mix
    and 3 ounces salt, or 3 ounces
    salt-based dry seafood boil (from
    grocery or specialty stores or
    online)
2 large onions, quartered

2 lemons, halved
3 pounds shrimp, 3 dozen crabs, or
    18–20 pounds crawfish
Salt and cayenne pepper
1½ pounds small red potatoes
6 ears corn on the cob

1. Bring enough water to cover seafood to a boil in a large pot (preferably outside over a propane or natural gas burner made for boiling seafood). Add crab boil, salt, onions, and lemons and bring to a boil. Add seafood. Bring water to a boil again.
2. Cover and turn off the heat. Shrimp will be cooked in 10 minutes, crawfish in 20 minutes, and crabs in 25–30 minutes. Scoop seafood out of water, draining well, and pile on the top of an outdoor picnic table covered with newspaper or onto serving trays. Sprinkle lightly with salt and cayenne, if desired.
3. Bring the seasoned water to a boil again. Add potatoes and cook 15 minutes. Scoop and drain potatoes. Add corn and cook 6 minutes. Drain and serve potatoes and corn with hot seafood.

Crawfish or Shrimp Étouffée

Makes 4 servings

Étouffée is the French word for smothered, and in this dish crawfish tails are smothered in onions and traditionally served over rice. Although many cooks in the area now add roux and tomatoes to étouffée, originally this dish did not have either. A little cornstarch is best to tighten the gravy, which should not be too thick. At my house, a salad of fresh cucumbers and tomatoes and hot bread always completes the meal.

1 pound crawfish tails or peeled and
    deveined shrimp
½ cup (1 stick) butter
1 cup chopped onion
½ cup chopped celery
½ cup chopped bell pepper
2 teaspoons finely chopped garlic

2 cups seafood or chicken broth
    or stock, divided
¾ teaspoon salt
¼ teaspoon ground black pepper
2 tablespoons cornstarch
Hot cooked rice for serving

1. If using frozen crawfish, thaw and soak in cold water 10 minutes. Drain and set aside.
2. Melt butter in a large skillet set over medium heat. Add onion, celery, bell pepper, and garlic. Cook, stirring occasionally, 10 minutes.
3. Add 1½ cups broth, salt, and pepper. Bring to a boil. Add crawfish and simmer 10 minutes.
4. In a small bowl, mix together cornstarch and remaining ½ cup broth. Stir into gravy. Simmer until sauce thickens, about 2 minutes. Adjust seasoning to taste. Serve hot over rice.

Crawfish Pasta

Makes 4 servings

My good friend Janet shared this simple but delicious recipe that she calls "Crawfish Elegance." It's another fine example of the creativity of our area cooks.

1 pound crawfish tails, defrosted if
    frozen
1 quart water
2 teaspoons dry crawfish or crab boil
    (from specialty stores or online)
12 tablespoons (1½ sticks) butter,
    divided
1 bunch green onions, chopped
½ cup chopped parsley

3 tablespoons all-purpose flour
1 pint half-and-half
3 ounces sherry
¾ teaspoon salt
¼ teaspoon cayenne or white pepper
¼ teaspoon garlic powder
French bread or cooked pasta for
    serving
Paprika for garnish

1. Rinse crawfish in cool water. Bring quart of water to a boil and add crawfish boil. Add crawfish, bring to a boil, and immediately remove from heat. Let sit 10 minutes. Drain and discard liquid.
2. Melt 6 tablespoons butter in a skillet set over medium-high heat. Add green onions, parsley, and crawfish. Sauté 6 minutes. Set aside.
3. In a 3-quart pot, melt remaining 6 tablespoons butter. Whisk in flour and cook, whisking constantly, to make a light roux, about the color of a cashew. Whisk in half-and-half. Cook on low heat 3 minutes.
4. Add crawfish mixture and continue cooking 5 minutes. Add sherry, salt, cayenne pepper, and garlic powder. Stir well, bring to boil, and remove from heat. Garnish with paprika. Serve hot with French bread or over pasta.

Crab Claw and Crawfish Salad

Makes 8 servings

The creative cooks on the German Coast can take the simplest food and turn it into something delicious, and this is one of those dishes. Handling live crawfish is a risky business. I once bought 20 pounds of live crawfish to prepare for my mom and dad. To purge the crawfish before boiling them, I put the whole 20 pounds in the kitchen sink in water and left the room a few minutes. When I got back, crawfish were crawling all over the floor.

1 pound large crawfish tails, defrosted if frozen
1 quart water
1 teaspoon dry or powdered salt-based crab boil (from specialty stores or online)
1 pound cooked crab claws (hard outer shells removed)

1 cup commercially prepared Italian olive salad
½ cup pickled vegetables
Salt and pepper to taste
Lettuce leaves and French bread or crackers for serving

1. Rinse crawfish tails in cool water. Bring 1 quart water to a boil in a large saucepan and add crab boil. Add crawfish, bring to a boil, and turn off heat. Let sit 10 minutes. Drain.
2. Place crawfish in a large bowl along with crab claws, olive salad, and pickled vegetables. Season with salt and pepper and mix well. Refrigerate until ready to serve.
3. For a quick lunch dish, serve on a lettuce leaf with a side of French bread. This is also good as an appetizer with crackers.

Seafood Salad

Makes 4–6 entrée salad servings

This simple recipe is great as an appetizer, salad, or sandwich filling. It's best made with fresh crabmeat or shrimp, or a combination of the two.

1 pound cooked crabmeat or peeled shrimp

3 hard-boiled eggs, chopped

¼ cup mayonnaise

3 tablespoons finely chopped celery

3 tablespoons finely chopped olives with pimento

2 tablespoons finely chopped dill pickle

1 teaspoon prepared yellow mustard

¼ teaspoon cayenne pepper

⅛ teaspoon garlic powder

Check crabmeat for small pieces of shell and remove. Place all ingredients in a bowl and mix gently. Cover and refrigerate until ready to serve.

Crab Cakes (or Stuffed Crabs)

Makes 12 small crab cakes, or stuffing for 8 crabs

We loved anything made with crab. Although most crab cakes are shaped like hockey pucks, we made ours flat like hamburger patties and served them on buttered buns. When crab cakes became available on virtually every restaurant's seafood menu, we did not see them as a gourmet item—we'd been eating them all our lives.

1 pound crabmeat, lump or claw
1 cup (2 sticks) butter, divided
¼ cup finely chopped celery
¼ cup finely chopped onion
1 teaspoon salt
½ teaspoon dried thyme
¼ teaspoon dried oregano

¼ teaspoon black pepper, or cayenne
  pepper to taste
2 slices white bread
1 large egg, slightly beaten
Tartar sauce (recipe page 99) and hot
  French bread for serving

1. Pick through crabmeat to remove small pieces of shell. Set aside.
2. Melt ½ cup butter in a 6-inch skillet over medium-high heat. Add celery and onion and sauté 10 minutes. Add salt, thyme, oregano, and pepper. Mix well. Remove from heat.
3. Place bread in a food processor and process to make fresh crumbs. Into onion mixture, stir in bread crumbs, egg, and crabmeat. Shape into 12 cakes, each about 2 inches in diameter and 1 inch thick. Refrigerate until ready to cook.
4. Melt remaining ½ cup butter in a large skillet set over medium heat. Fry crab cakes until browned on each side. Serve with tartar sauce and hot buttered French bread.

Stuffed Crabs

Lightly pack 2 ounces of crab cake stuffing into a dozen cleaned and prepared crab shells or aluminum ramekins. Top with buttered bread crumbs. Bake at 350°F for 15 minutes.

Boiled Crab Stew

Makes 6 servings

Using leftover boiled crabs for a stew adds a depth of flavor that cannot be duplicated by adding liquid crab boil to the dish. Mama kept a patch of parsley near the back door of the kitchen, and she always finished this stew with a handful of chopped parsley. Picking the meat out of a crab at the dinner table is a messy job, and the gravy might trickle down your arm, but who cares? This dish is that good.

6 large boiled crabs or 1 pound
   crabmeat
½ cup vegetable oil
½ cup all-purpose flour
1 cup chopped onion
½ cup chopped celery
2 cloves garlic, mashed

1 teaspoon salt
6 cups seafood broth, chicken broth,
   or water
2 tablespoons chopped parsley
Hot cooked rice or mashed potatoes
   for serving

1. Remove the back shell, lungs, and other inedible parts of the crabs and discard. Break each body in two. Set crab bodies and claws aside.
2. In a large, heavy-bottomed saucepan set over medium heat, add oil and flour. Make a dark roux by stirring mixture constantly until dark brown, about 10 minutes. Add onion, celery, garlic, and salt. Cook 10 minutes, stirring constantly.
3. Add broken crabs, claws, and broth. Bring to a boil, reduce heat, and simmer 20 minutes. Stir in parsley and adjust seasoning to taste. Serve hot over rice or mashed potatoes, and with plenty of napkins.

Fried Soft-Shell Crabs

Makes 4 servings

The soft-shell crab industry is thriving on the German Coast, but working at such a job is demanding. During the molting process, crabs must be watched constantly so that they can be plucked from the water at just the right moment. Lucky for us, there are people willing to keep vigils over crabs. In my opinion, there is nothing as delicious as a perfectly fried soft-shell crab. With soft-shells, you eat the whole crab, shell and all. I like them on sandwiches or with tartar sauce and a side of French fries.

Vegetable oil for frying
8 large soft-shell crabs
Salt
Pepper
3 cups commercial fish fry or
    seasoned flour (Add ½ teaspoon
    salt and ¼ teaspoon black pepper
    to each cup of flour.)

2 large eggs
¾ cup water
Tartar sauce (recipe page 99) and hot
    French bread for serving

1. In a deep fryer, heat 2 inches oil to 360°F. Clean crabs by first removing the apron underneath the crab. Turn back each end of the crab's top shell and remove the spongy lumps, sand bag, and gills from underneath. Snip off eyes and mouth. Rinse with cold water and pat dry inside and outside.
2. Lightly season crabs with salt and pepper. Add fish fry to a large, shallow bowl. In a separate shallow bowl, whisk together eggs and water. Dredge each crab in fish fry, dip in egg wash, and dredge again in fish fry.
3. Fry 2 crabs at a time until golden brown on both sides, about 8–10 minutes total. Serve hot with tartar sauce and French bread, and either make a sandwich or eat crabs and bread separately.

Note: Oysters and shrimp can be fried using the same method.

Crabmeat Au Gratin

Makes 4–6 servings

1 pound crabmeat
½ cup finely chopped onion
½ cup finely chopped celery
¼ cup chopped green onions
½ cup (1 stick) unsalted butter
½ cup all-purpose flour
1 (13-ounce) can evaporated milk

2 egg yolks, slightly beaten
1 teaspoon salt
¼ teaspoon ground black pepper
¼ teaspoon cayenne pepper
¼ teaspoon freshly grated nutmeg
½ pound Cheddar cheese, grated

1. Preheat oven to 375°F. Check crabmeat for pieces of shell and remove.
2. In a large skillet set over medium-high heat, sauté onion, celery, and green onions in melted butter 5 minutes. Blend in flour. Gradually add milk, whisking constantly. Bring to a boil over medium heat. Lower heat and stir in egg yolks, salt, peppers, and nutmeg.
3. Divide crabmeat among heatproof serving dishes or ramekins, or place in a buttered casserole dish. Top with sauce, then cheese. Bake until cheese is melted and sauce is bubbly, about 20 minutes. Let sit at least 5 minutes and serve warm.

Oyster Cocktail

Makes 4 servings

Right before Thanksgiving, Mama would buy a sack of oysters on the pretext that she needed some for her turkey dressing. She and my brother shucked the oysters under a tree in the backyard, and I think they ate more of them raw than what was kept for oyster dressing. Right from the shell, they slurped them down. No beer or sauce, just oysters and the juice. I can still hear them raving about how big or small or salty those oysters were.

1 cup tomato sauce or catsup
½ cup freshly squeezed lemon juice
¼ cup finely chopped celery

2½ tablespoons prepared horseradish
Tabasco sauce to taste
1 dozen oysters, freshly shucked

Place all ingredients, except oysters, in a pint jar. Cover and shake well. Store in the refrigerator up to 2 days. To serve, put 3 cold, raw oysters in a fancy cocktail glass and top with sauce.

Note: Also good with boiled shrimp.

Oysters Mosca
Makes 8 servings

People here love replicating iconic dishes. Oysters Mosca is rightfully famous, and it was created at Mosca's, an old-line Italian restaurant on Highway 90 near Waggaman, halfway between the German Coast and New Orleans. Here is my version.

1 quart oysters, drained
1 tablespoon chopped parsley
2 teaspoons freshly squeezed lemon
    juice
½ teaspoon salt
¼ teaspoon ground black pepper

1½ cups Italian bread crumbs
½ cup freshly grated Parmesan
    cheese
6 tablespoons (¾ stick) unsalted
    butter, melted

1. Preheat oven to 325°F. Grease a 9×13-inch baking dish with olive oil.
2. Place oysters in a single layer in prepared dish. Sprinkle on parsley, lemon juice, salt, and pepper. Top with bread crumbs and cheese.
3. Pour butter evenly over everything. Bake until golden brown and crusty, about 35 minutes. Serve hot.

Pecan Catfish

Makes 6 servings

People on the German Coast didn't always have to go to a grocery store to get the things they needed for a great meal. Catfish were plentiful in the Mississippi River, in nearby Lac des Allemands, and in the bayous. Just about everyone had a pecan tree in their yard, and if you didn't have a Meyer lemon tree, your neighbor probably did.

6 (7-ounce) catfish filets
3 cups shelled pecans
1 cup plain bread crumbs
3 large eggs
½ cup whole milk

1 cup all-purpose flour
2 teaspoons salt
1 teaspoon ground black pepper
1 stick butter or ½ cup corn oil
Lemon wedges for serving

1. Preheat oven to 200°F. Wash and trim catfish filets. Place in refrigerator.
2. Place pecans in a single layer on a cookie sheet. Bake 10 minutes. Finely chop pecans in a food processor. Transfer to a large, shallow bowl. Add bread crumbs and mix well.
3. Stir together eggs and milk in another bowl. In a third bowl, combine flour, salt, and pepper.
4. Bread chilled filets by first dredging them in seasoned flour, then dipping them in egg wash, and then dredging in pecan mixture. Refrigerate until ready to fry.
5. Heat butter in a large skillet set over medium heat. Pan-fry breaded fish until brown on one side; then turn fish over to brown second side. Place on a cooling rack positioned on a baking sheet in oven while frying remainder of the filets. Serve with lemon wedges.

Fish Court Bouillon

Makes 4–6 servings

This is another dish popular with fishermen in the area. Barely resembling the pale, thin court bouillon found in France, our thick, tomato-red court bouillon is served in a bowl with rice. It can be a thick soup or a stew, depending on the texture of the gravy.

1 cup (2 sticks) unsalted butter
1 cup all-purpose flour
1½ cups finely chopped onion
½ cup finely chopped bell pepper
1 cup finely chopped celery
2 cloves garlic, mashed
1 (4-ounce) can tomato paste

1 (8-ounce) can tomato sauce
2½ teaspoons Creole seasoning
1 quart water or fish stock
1 tablespoon Worcestershire sauce
1 lemon, sliced
3 pounds cleaned redfish or catfish
Hot cooked rice for serving

1. Melt butter in a 5-quart Dutch oven set over medium heat. Add flour and stir constantly to make a medium-colored roux.
2. Add onion, bell pepper, celery, and garlic. Lower heat and cook 10 minutes, stirring constantly. Add tomato paste, tomato sauce, and Creole seasoning. Cook an additional 15 minutes.
3. Add water, Worcestershire sauce, and lemon slices. Bring to a boil, then lower heat; simmer, uncovered, 1 hour or until sauce thickens. Stir occasionally.
4. Cut fish into 2-inch chunks and drop into court bouillon. Bring to a boil, lower heat, cover, and cook until fish turns white and flaky. Serve hot over rice.

Stuffed Flounder

Makes 6 servings

Mama and Daddy loved stuffed flounder. This was a dish they first ordered in a restaurant, fell in love with, and later duplicated at home. Stuffed flounder is quick to prepare, and Mama always served it with mashed potatoes.

6 medium-sized flounders, cleaned and scaled
½ cup finely chopped celery
½ cup finely chopped onion
¼ cup chopped green onions
3 tablespoons chopped parsley
2 cloves garlic, mashed
7 tablespoons butter, divided

1 pound shrimp, peeled and deveined
½ pound crabmeat
1 cup bread crumbs, divided
3 large egg yolks
½ teaspoon salt-based liquid crab boil (from specialty stores or online)
Salt and ground black pepper

1. Preheat oven to 350°F. Cut top side of flounder down the middle along the spine. With the tip of a knife, gently lift meat off bones on both sides. Remove as many bones as possible. Wash fish and pat dry.
2. In a large skillet over medium heat, sauté celery, onion, green onions, parsley, and garlic in 3 tablespoons melted butter 5 minutes. Add shrimp and cook until shrimp turn pink. Gently stir in crabmeat, ½ cup bread crumbs, egg yolks, crab boil, and ½ teaspoon salt.
3. Melt remaining 4 tablespoons butter and brush onto the insides of flounder. Season inside and outside of fish with salt and pepper.
4. Place equal portions of stuffing inside the top openings of each fish. Pull sides up to surround stuffing. Top with remaining ½ cup bread crumbs. Brush with butter. Bake until fish is flaky and stuffing is brown, approximately 20 minutes. Serve hot.

Baked Red Snapper or Redfish

Makes 6–8 servings

This was another dish my mom always served with mashed potatoes. It is outstanding, but watch out for tiny bones.

1 (4–5-pound) red snapper or
    redfish, cleaned and scaled
2 lemons, divided
½ teaspoon salt
¼ teaspoon ground black pepper
3 tablespoons salted butter
2 tablespoons all-purpose flour
1 (1-pound) can whole chopped
    tomatoes, with liquid

1 bell pepper, chopped
¾ cup chopped onion
½ cup chopped celery
¼ cup chopped green onions
2 bay leaves
1 cup hot water
2 bay leaves
1 pound shrimp, peeled and deveined
1 pound crabmeat (check for shells)

1. Season fish with the juice of one lemon, salt, and pepper.
2. Melt butter over medium heat in a heavy skillet. Add flour and cook, stirring constantly, 3 minutes. Add tomatoes and their liquid, bell pepper, onion, celery, green onions, bay leaves, and hot water. Bring to a boil, reduce heat, and simmer, uncovered, 20 minutes. Remove bay leaves.
3. Place fish in a large, rimmed baking pan. Top with shrimp, crabmeat, and sauce.
4. Slice remaining lemon. Place on top of fish. Cover and bake until fish is flaky and cooked through, about 45 minutes. Serve hot.

Fried Seafood with Tartar Sauce

Makes 6–8 servings

This breading mix can be used on a variety of seafood, including fish, shrimp, and oysters. Originally, most people on the German Coast breaded seafood with seasoned cornmeal. Today, many people use a 50-50 combination of cornmeal and corn flour. You can certainly fry your seafood in an electric fryer, but I like to use my large, cast-iron Dutch oven, as my mother did.

2–3 pounds catfish, shrimp, or
    oysters, cleaned and dressed
Vegetable oil for frying

Tartar sauce for serving (*recipe follows*), or cocktail sauce

Egg Wash

2 eggs
1 cup water
3 tablespoons yellow mustard

2 teaspoons lemon juice
½ teaspoon garlic powder
Salt and black pepper to taste

Cornmeal Mix

2 cups cornmeal
2 cups corn flour
4 teaspoons salt

1 teaspoon ground black pepper
½ teaspoon cayenne pepper

1. Combine all ingredients for egg wash in a 2-quart casserole dish. Combine all ingredients for cornmeal mix in another large, shallow container.
2. Wash fish and pat dry. Heat 1½ inches oil in a fryer or heavy Dutch oven to 360°F.
3. Dip seafood into egg wash, then dredge in cornmeal mix.
4. Drop into hot oil, being careful not to overload the pot. Fry until seafood floats and is golden brown. Remove from oil and drain on paper towels. Serve hot with tartar or cocktail sauce, or use to make a poor boy.

Tartar Sauce
Makes 1 pint

Friday night was our time for fried seafood, which was always served with homemade tartar sauce and hot French bread.

1½ cups mayonnaise
1 cup finely chopped dill pickles
2 cloves garlic, finely minced

2 teaspoons freshly squeezed lemon
juice

Mix ingredients in a glass pint jar. Store in refrigerator until ready to use. Keeps up to 1 week.

My mama's four sisters were all good cooks. So were her three brothers, although they were never allowed in the kitchen when Mam Papaul and Mémère were cooking.

Four generations of women in my family, including (*from left, standing*) Mémère, Mam Papaul, Lelia, her four sisters, and three sisters-in-law. I am sitting with my chin in my hand.

Codfish Cakes

Makes 4–6 servings

Even though codfish don't live in Louisiana's waters, codfish cakes were a favorite Lenten dish at my house. Many cooks make fish cakes with raw onions, but I like to cook the onions before adding them to the potatoes.

½ cup oil for frying
¼ cup finely chopped onion
¼ cup chopped green onions
2 tablespoons butter
2 cups mashed potatoes
7 ounces canned codfish flakes,
    rinsed and drained

1 large egg
¼ cup chopped parsley
½ teaspoon salt
¼ teaspoon ground black pepper
¾ cup all-purpose flour

1. Preheat oil in a fryer or skillet to 350°F. In a separate skillet over medium-high heat, sauté onion and green onions in butter until tender. Remove skillet from heat; add potatoes, fish flakes, egg, parsley, salt, and pepper and mix well.
2. Divide mixture into 8 portions and shape the portions into patties. Flour both sides of each patty and fry in hot oil until both sides are golden brown and crisp, about 2–3 minutes per side. Drain on paper towels and serve hot. (Mixture can also be baked in a buttered 1-quart casserole at 350°F for 30 minutes.)

5

Salads and Vegetables

VEGETABLE GARDENS WERE extremely important to the early settlers on Louisiana's German Coast. My grandfather, Ulysses Tregre, was German and the descendant of one of the original colonists of the German Coast. He was born in 1868 and was the father of nine children. Unfortunately, my grandmother Magdelene Angelle (Granier) Tregre died at age thirty-six, and my grandfather lived to the age of ninety-four as a widower. He was a plantation overseer, and at various times, his family lived on Gold Mine, Evergreen, and Whitney Plantations. With his large family to feed, "making a garden" was important. Fortunately, he had a green thumb, and he grew beautiful mirlitons, a variety of beans and peas, cabbage, greens, beets, eggplant, and okra. Growing vegetables not only provided food, but it taught his boys the value of hard work and perseverance.

The alluvial soil deposited in our area from the annual overflowing of the Mississippi River (before we had levees) still serves us well and is excellent for growing produce such as greens, shallots, onions, and a variety of squashes and root vegetables. As in my grandfather's garden, we also grew beans, peas, and cabbage.

Anyone who grows a serious garden must have a wheelbarrow,
and mine is one of my prized possessions. It is made from the wheel and
side support rails that my grandfather Ulysses gave my dad when I was young.
I don't remember the conversation from that day, but I do remember the tone;
my grandfather was giving my dad something very special. The wheel and rails were
probably given to him by his father. Gardening equipment was extremely
expensive way back when, and a wheelbarrow was a necessity.

~ SALADS ~

Fresh Beet Salad
Makes 4–6 servings

Beets were one of the root vegetables my dad always planted. I don't remember him eating them, but they certainly were one of my mom's favorite vegetables.

3 tablespoons light olive or vegetable
    oil
2 tablespoons cider vinegar
Salt and ground black pepper to taste

4 medium-sized raw beets
2 hard-boiled eggs, sliced
1 small red onion, thinly sliced

1. Make salad dressing by whisking together oil, vinegar, salt, and black pepper. Set aside.
2. Place beets in a 5-quart pot and cover with water. Bring to a boil. Lower heat and cook until tender, 45–60 minutes. Drain and peel beets with your hands; the outer skins will slide right off.
3. Slice beets and arrange on a platter with eggs and onion. Drizzle dressing over everything and serve warm or at room temperature.

Creole Tomato and Cucumber Salad
Makes 4–6 servings

There isn't anything much better than a salad of fresh Creole tomatoes during tomato season, June to August. The tomatoes grown on the German Coast have a distinctive flavor and are sought after by chefs in New Orleans, as well as by locals. My sister Dale married James Zeringue, who is descended from the Zeringue brothers who arrived on the German Coast in 1721. Their family farm of more than two hundred acres has developed a reputation for producing some of the best tomatoes in the area. Each summer, people drive from miles around to buy them by the basket.

Strangely, when I was young, although cucumbers grew on the back fence near my father's garden, we weren't allowed to eat them. Daddy said cucumbers were horse food. Something from his childhood? We didn't have horses in the backyard, so those cucumbers would go to waste. When I'm having only a cucumber salad today, I often just douse it with rice vinegar instead of traditional cider vinegar. I prefer rice vinegar because it has a mild, sweet taste.

Most of our salads when I was a child were very simple. Other than mayonnaise, our one and only salad dressing was made from olive oil and vinegar.

4 large Creole tomatoes, sliced
1 medium cucumber, peeled and
    sliced
1 small red onion, thinly sliced

⅓ cup olive oil
2 tablespoons cider vinegar
Salt and ground black pepper to taste

1. Arrange tomato and cucumber slices on a platter. Top with red onions.
2. Mix oil, vinegar, salt, and pepper. Pour over vegetables and serve.

Mirliton Salad

Makes 4–8 servings

The humble mirliton can be enjoyed in everything from salad to desserts. My uncle Clancy Faucheux, who retired from the army, spent time in Korea, where he found mirlitons growing in the wild. While there, he put his culinary skills to work and cooked those wild mirlitons with shrimp, just as his mother had prepared them back in Hahnville. His fellow soldiers thought the dish was fantastic.

4 medium mirlitons
1 teaspoon salt
⅓ cup vegetable oil
2 tablespoons vinegar

¼ teaspoon garlic powder
¼ teaspoon onion powder
Salt and ground black pepper to taste

1. Peel and dice mirlitons. Place in a large pot and add salt and enough water to cover. Bring to a boil and lower to a simmer. Cook until tender, about 20 minutes.
2. In a small bowl, mix together oil, vinegar, garlic powder, and onion powder. Pour over mirliton pieces. Serve as a hot or cold salad.

Mam Papaul's Potato Salad

Makes 4–6 servings

On Sundays, Mam Papaul never knew who or how many would show up for noon dinner. Everyone was welcomed graciously, whether they had been invited or not. Potato salad was usually on the menu, especially if we were eating gumbo. Whoever made the potato salad gave the mayonnaise her undivided attention. That cook was also always expected to "do a few more" potatoes at the last minute, when unexpected relatives dropped in.

4 large russet potatoes
3 hard-boiled eggs, chopped
¾ cup mayonnaise, commercial or homemade (*recipe follows*)
⅓ cup finely chopped dill pickles

⅓ cup finely chopped celery
¼ cup chopped olives with pimento
½ teaspoon prepared yellow mustard
Salt and ground black pepper to taste

1. Peel, dice, and boil potatoes until just tender. (Boil them too much and they will mash.) Cool. You should have around 4 cups diced potatoes.
2. In a large bowl, gently mix together all ingredients. Cover and refrigerate until ready to serve.

Homemade Mayonnaise

Makes 1 cup

Use a hand mixer or blender to make this mayonnaise. This cannot be hurried; be patient and add oil a little at a time.

1 raw egg, preferably a yard egg, or the yolks of two hard-boiled eggs*
1 cup salad oil
2 teaspoons lemon juice

¼ teaspoon salt
¼ teaspoon ground black pepper, or cayenne to taste
1 squirt yellow mustard

1. Using a hand mixer or blender, beat egg on low speed until very light and lemon colored, about 30 seconds.
2. Add salad oil 2 teaspoons at a time, beating well on low speed after each addition. When all oil has been added, mayonnaise should be glossy and hold its shape when lifted with a spoon.

3. Season with lemon juice, salt, pepper, and mustard. Taste and adjust seasoning. Store in a covered container in refrigerator.

*My aunt Adeline (pronounced Ad-leen) made her mayonnaise with hard-boiled egg yolks, and it always turned out perfectly. For me, however, it's much easier to make with a raw egg.

German Potato Salad

Makes 6 servings

This recipe is based on the one my aunt Audrey Voekel Faucheux made occasionally for Sunday dinner at my grandmother's house. It has completely ruined us because we are now torn between our traditional potato salad and this "German" one. I have made the decision to maintain Mam Papaul's recipe as our gumbo potato salad, and I serve this one for other special occasions.

10 strips bacon	⅓ cup vinegar
18 new potatoes	2 teaspoons cornstarch
1 large onion, coarsely chopped	1 teaspoon sugar
3 tablespoons water	Salt and ground black pepper

1. In a large skillet, fry bacon over medium heat until crisp. Remove bacon from skillet, coarsely chop, and set aside. Retain bacon grease in pan.
2. Boil potatoes until tender. Do not remove skin. Drain and slice.
3. Add onion to the bacon grease and cook over medium heat until light brown.
4. Deglaze pan with water. Add vinegar, cornstarch, and sugar to pan. Cook over low heat until slightly thick, about 3 minutes. Place potatoes on a serving platter. Top with onion and bacon. Season lightly with salt and black pepper. Drizzle with the warm vinegar dressing. Serve warm.

~ VEGETABLES ~

Artichoke Casserole

Makes 9 servings

This recipe can be made into balls and baked at 350°F for 10–12 minutes.

2 pounds ground beef
1 (12-ounce) jar marinated artichoke
    hearts, mashed, retaining liquid
1½ cups Italian bread crumbs
½ cup grated Parmesan cheese

½ cup water
1 large egg, lightly beaten
3 tablespoons olive oil
2 teaspoons minced garlic

Preheat oven to 350°F. Brown ground beef in a skillet set over medium-high heat. Drain well. Mix in remaining ingredients and spoon into an 8×8-inch casserole dish. Bake until top is bubbly and brown, about 25 minutes. Let sit at least 5 minutes. Serve warm.

Fried Broccoli and Cauliflower

Makes 6 servings

Broccoli and cauliflower fried in Italian bread crumbs is a favorite with my children, who think of themselves as more Italian than French or German. It is a favorite with the Italians who settled on the German Coast. My husband, Charles, is of Sicilian and Scots descent, but mostly Sicilian. It seems that Charles's Italian grandparents made their living selling and preparing food. His grandfather was a fisherman in Sicily, as well as in the United States. His Italian grandmother owned a grocery store and then a boardinghouse in Beaumont, Texas.

Vegetable oil for frying
12 broccoli florets, stemmed
12 cauliflower florets
2 large eggs

2 tablespoons water
2 cups Italian bread crumbs
Salt and ground black pepper

1. In a heavy skillet, preheat 1 inch oil to 360°F. Meanwhile, parboil broccoli and cauliflower 2 minutes. Rinse in cold water and drain well.

2. In a small bowl, whisk eggs with water. Pour bread crumbs into a shallow bowl. Roll vegetables in bread crumbs, dip in egg wash, then roll again in bread crumbs.
3. Fry in hot oil until golden brown. Drain. Sprinkle with salt and pepper. Serve hot.

Holiday Green Bean Casserole
Makes 4–6 servings

I am not a fan of canned soups, but this dish is so good I must share it. This recipe brings accolades to the table each time I make it. One night I took this dish to a Lions Club supper, and as I sat down, a friend turned to me and said, "Have you tasted those green beans from that table over there? They are delicious." Yes, they were my green beans.

½ cup (1 stick) butter
½ cup chopped onion
1 (15-ounce) can cream of mushroom soup
30 Ritz-type crackers, crushed

8 ounces sharp cheddar cheese, grated
2 (14-ounce) cans French-style green beans, drained
8 thin slices andouille or smoked pork sausage

1. Preheat oven to 350°F. Melt butter in a large skillet set over medium-high heat and sauté onion until light brown, about 6 minutes. Add mushroom soup and mix well.
2. Mix crushed crackers and cheese together and set aside.
3. Spread ½ of beans on bottom of a 2-quart ovenproof dish. Top with ½ of mushroom soup mixture, then with half of cracker mixture. Repeat layers. Arrange andouille slices on top of everything. Bake until bubbly and brown, about 30 minutes. Let cool 10 minutes and serve warm.

Smothered Green Beans and New Potatoes

Makes 4–6 servings

When I was a child, just about everyone had long green beans growing in their garden. We called them string beans or snap beans. One of my tasks during the summer was to pull off the fibrous strings that ran the length of the beans, snip the tips off, and cut them into 2-inch pieces. We always cooked string beans with pickled pork and new potatoes. "Smothering" is a term we use when we put vegetables in a covered pot and slowly cook them until they're extremely tender, usually with seasoning meat.

2 pounds fresh green beans
½ cup chopped onion
2 tablespoons vegetable oil or bacon grease

1 pound new potatoes, scrubbed and quartered
½ pound pickle meat (pickled pork)
½ cup water
Salt and ground black pepper to taste

1. Tip beans (cut off the hard ends) and remove the strings. Cut into 2-inch pieces. Set aside.
2. In a 3-quart saucepan set over medium heat, sauté onion in oil 10 minutes, stirring constantly.
3. Add beans to pot and cook on medium heat with onion until beans are just tender. Add potatoes, meat, and water.
4. Cover and cook on medium heat until potatoes are tender and green beans are limp and tender, about 30–35 minutes. You have now smothered your veggies! Season with salt and pepper.

Butter Beans with Shrimp

Makes 6–8 servings

This dish has been cooked on the German Coast for as long as anyone can remember. Rarely does it appear on a menu outside the mom-and-pop restaurants along our stretch of the Mississippi River. Most people call these beans "limas," but we always call them "butter beans," no matter the size. We typically make this treat in the summer, when both shrimp and vegetables are plentiful.

½ cup all-purpose flour
½ cup vegetable oil
¾ cup chopped onion
2 cloves garlic, minced
1½ pounds fresh or frozen baby lima beans
5 cups water or unseasoned shrimp stock

2 teaspoons salt
½ teaspoon ground black pepper
1 pound small peeled shrimp (60–80 count)
2 green onions, chopped
¼ cup chopped parsley
Hot cooked rice for serving

1. In a large, heavy-bottomed saucepan set over medium heat, add flour and oil and stir constantly to make a medium-brown roux, the color of peanut butter.
2. Add onion and garlic. Lower heat and cook, stirring constantly, 10 minutes.
3. Add lima beans, water or stock, salt, and black pepper. Stir to dissolve roux. Bring to a boil, then lower heat and simmer until beans are tender, about 20 minutes.
4. Add shrimp, green onions, and parsley. Bring to a boil. Lower heat and simmer until shrimp turn pink, about 5 minutes. Thin sauce with water or stock if desired. Adjust seasoning to taste and serve warm over rice.

New Year's Day Black-Eyed Peas

Makes 8 servings

We always had black-eyed peas and cabbage on New Year's Day for good luck and prosperity. Purple hull peas and field peas are also good cooked this way.

1 pound dried black-eyed peas
6–8 cups water
½ pound link smoked sausage and/or
   a hambone
1 cup chopped onion
1 cup chopped celery

1 clove garlic, minced
1 cup fresh green beans, trimmed
   and cut into 2-inch pieces
   (optional)
Salt and ground black pepper to taste
Hot cooked rice for serving

1. Rinse and drain black-eyed peas. Place in a 5-quart pot along with 6 cups water, sausage, onion, celery, and garlic. Bring to a boil. Lower heat and simmer, covered, until peas are tender, about 45 to 60 minutes. If water gets low, add more.
2. Add green beans and cook a few more minutes, uncovered, until green beans are tender. When finished, liquid should be creamy. Remove sausage, slice, and place back in bean pot. Season with salt and pepper and serve warm over rice.

Monday Red Bean Dinner

Makes 8 servings

This recipe differs from red bean gumbo in that it is thicker and is not made with roux. If we were still living in the early twentieth century, this is a dish that could simmer on the stove while the laundry was being washed in the outdoor wash shed. Everyone had a wash shed along with an outhouse and clothesline in the backyard.

1 pound dried red beans
8 cups water
1 meaty hambone or 1 pound
   smoked sausage
1 large onion, chopped

½ cup chopped celery
¼ cup chopped bell pepper
2 cloves garlic, minced
Salt and ground black pepper
Cooked rice for serving

1. Rinse and drain beans. Place in a 5-quart pot along with water, hambone, onion, celery, bell pepper, and garlic. Cover, bring to a boil, then remove cover, lower heat, and cook until beans are tender, which can take up to 3 hours. Stir occasionally. If water gets low, stir in 1 cup more at a time.
2. When beans are tender and creamy, season with salt and black pepper to taste. Slice sausage and serve with the beans hot over rice.

White Beans with Ham

Makes 8 servings

White beans, sometimes called navy beans, were the favorite bean at our house. My mom always cooked them with a hambone. She would take that bone and scoop out the marrow and eat it. When making this recipe, buy fresh or newly picked beans if you can. They cook faster than old beans.

1 pound dried white (navy) beans
1 meaty hambone or 1 pound pickle
   meat (pickled pork)
8 cups water
1 large onion, chopped

½ cup chopped celery
2 cloves garlic, minced
Salt and ground black pepper
Cooked rice for serving

1. Rinse and drain beans. Place in a 5-quart pot along with hambone, water, onion, celery, and garlic. Cover and bring to a boil. Lower to a simmer and cook, uncovered, until beans are tender, about 3 hours. Stir occasionally. If water gets low, stir in 1 cup more at a time.
2. When beans are tender and creamy, season with salt and black pepper to taste. Serve hot over rice.

Petit Pois with a Little Roux
Makes 6 servings

I remember this dish from visits more than sixty-five years ago to my pépère and aunt Hedwidge's house in Wallace. Those were days of running after blackbirds, sitting on the floor in front of the fireplace warming my hands and backside, picking pecans in the backyard, and walking outdoors to the outhouse in time of need.

3 slices bacon
2 tablespoons all-purpose flour
3 tablespoons chopped onion
1 cup water or milk, if using frozen
   peas

2 cups frozen peas, cooked and
   drained, or 1 (16-ounce) can tiny
   green peas, with liquid
Salt and ground black pepper to taste
Cooked rice or baked pastry shells
   for serving

1. In a large saucepan, fry bacon over medium heat until crisp. Crumble and set aside. Leave grease in pan.
2. Add flour to bacon grease and cook, stirring constantly, to make a roux the color of a copper penny. Add onion and cook, stirring constantly, 3 minutes. If using frozen peas, gradually whisk in water. Stir and cook until thickened.
4. Stir in peas, salt, and pepper. Serve hot over rice or in baked pastry shells. Garnish with crumbled bacon.

Aunt Hedwidge loved her old black cast-iron wood-burning stove.
I was always fascinated with the glow of the fire as she stoked the coals when
she baked in the oven. When one of her brothers bought her a gas stove,
she hesitated to use it, fearing she would blow up the house.

Smothered Cabbage and Pork

Makes 6 servings

This was one of my grandfather Leopold Faucheux's favorite dishes. Unlike the modern trend of steaming until tender-crisp, we always cooked our cabbage until it was limp and brown. It was so good cooked with spare ribs or pork chops. Some people cooked cabbage with oysters this very same way.

1 medium cabbage
1-pound rack pork spare ribs, or 4
    end-cut, bone-in pork chops
½ cup vegetable oil

1 cup chopped onion
1 cup water
Salt and ground black pepper to taste

1. Core and chop cabbage. Wash and drain.
2. Cut pork into individual ribs. Heat oil in a skillet set over medium-high heat and brown meat well. Remove ribs and set aside. Cook onions in same pot until brown, about 7 minutes.
3. Add cabbage, meat, and water. Stirring occasionally, cook until cabbage is limp and brown, about 40 minutes. Season with salt and pepper. Serve hot.

Sauerkraut

Makes about 2 gallons

Even though our area grows lots of cabbage and we have a strong German heritage, unfortunately, hardly anyone makes sauerkraut. I recently spoke with a few cousins in their late eighties, and they, until a few years ago, did make their own sauerkraut. My cousin Wayne Schexnayder, who owns Schexnayder's Acadian Foods, used to make a delicious sauerkraut that he served with kielbasa at our local church fairs. Although my mom owned a sauerkraut crock, she mainly used it to store lard. Once she did try to make sauerkraut, but it looked and smelled so bad that she threw it out and never attempted to make it again. I have since learned that scum can be removed from the top of fermenting sauerkraut and that the sauerkraut itself will be fine. The following recipe is the way I make sauerkraut today.

10 pounds cabbage, with cores and heavy ribs removed

8 ounces canning salt

11 quart-size sterilized canning jars with lids and screw tops (Each jar will hold 14–16 ounces kraut.)

1. Using a mandolin or very sharp knife, thinly shred cabbage. Place cabbage and salt in a large crock or nonreactive metal container. Mix well and let stand 2 hours.

2. Squeeze the cabbage with your hands until the cabbage is limp and has released its juices. Pound the cabbage into the vessel so that it sits tightly together. Place a large plate on top of the cabbage and place clean weights on the plate to keep the cabbage completely submerged. (If you don't have enough liquid to cover the cabbage, make additional brine by dissolving 1½ tablespoons canning salt in 1 quart water.) Cover the crock with a cloth and let it ferment in a warm area at least a month and up to 6 months, depending on how tart you like it. Sauerkraut will keep in the refrigerator from 6 months to a year.

3. To can, bring sauerkraut to a simmer, but do not boil. Pack into sterilized jars, adding enough sauerkraut brine to cover, leaving ½-inch head space. Be sure that rims of jars and lids are sterile. Put lids on jars loosely and place jars into a large pot or roaster. Add enough cold water to reach 2 inches above the top of the jars. Cover, bring to a boil, and boil 20 minutes, or place in a preheated 375°F degree oven for 20 minutes. Remove jars from hot water. Tighten lids, test for seals, and place in a dark, cool area up to a year.

Easy Sauerkraut

Makes 6 quarts

6 quarts finely sliced cabbage leaves
6 sterilized quart-size canning jars,
   with lids and screw tops

3 tablespoons sea salt or canning salt
Boiling water

1. Pack cabbage into jars. Add 1½ teaspoons salt to each jar.
2. Fill jars with boiling water. Be sure that water reaches the bottom of the jars and completely covers the top of the cabbage. Cover with sterilized lids and screw tops, making sure they are not tight. Set in a cool place for 2 weeks, and it's ready to serve. Store jars in the refrigerator up to a year.

Sauerkraut Cooked with Onions

Makes 6 servings

My aunt Gertrude made sauerkraut, but unfortunately her daughter Gert did not keep her recipe. The family used to make this simple dish using Aunt Gertrude's homemade sauerkraut.

1 quart fermented sauerkraut
2 tablespoons butter

1 large onion, coarsely chopped
Ground black pepper (optional)

1. Place sauerkraut in a large sieve or colander. Rinse with cold water and drain well.
2. Melt butter over medium-high heat in a large skillet. Add onion and sauté until just starting to turn brown, about 8–10 minutes. Add sauerkraut and cook until heated, stirring constantly. Season with black pepper and serve hot.

Hot Cabbage Slaw with Bacon

Makes 6 servings

I developed this recipe to use up an abundance of cabbage we caught at a St. Patrick's Day parade. It soon became a family favorite.

1 medium head cabbage
2 slices bacon
1 small onion, chopped

1 teaspoon freshly squeezed lemon
   juice
Salt and ground black pepper to taste

1. Core and finely shred cabbage. Rinse, drain, and set aside.
2. Cut bacon into small pieces and put into a skillet. Turn heat to medium and fry bacon until crisp. Remove from pan, leaving in grease.
3. Add onion to pan and cook 3 minutes, stirring constantly. Add cabbage, turn heat to medium-high, and stir-fry until tender but still crisp. Add reserved bacon and lemon juice. Season with salt and pepper. Stir well and serve hot.

Honey and Mint Glazed Carrots

Makes 4 servings

We grew carrots in the backyard, while others kept gardens on the levee near the river. Honey came from a neighbor's beehive, and mint grew wild in our yard near the cistern. Although we didn't drink mint juleps, we did enjoy mint in our tea, in lemonade, and in this dish.

12 tender young carrots, tops
   removed
4 tablespoons honey

2 tablespoons butter, melted
2 teaspoons very finely chopped
   mint leaves

1. Boil carrots until tender crisp. Drain and place in a serving dish.
2. Drizzle honey and butter over carrots. Top with mint. Serve warm.

Piggy Carrots

Makes 4–6 servings

If ever there was an heirloom recipe, it is this thrifty, nutritious, and delicious pork and carrot dish. I first tasted it at a Knights of Columbus supper, where I tracked down the little old lady who brought it. She couldn't give me a recipe, but she did tell me how she made this dish. This is my version.

2 pounds fresh carrots
1 pound seasoned bulk pork sausage
½ cup chopped onion
2 green onions, chopped

¼ cup chopped parsley
2 cloves garlic, finely minced
Salt and ground black pepper

1. Wash, peel, and cut carrots into 1-inch pieces. Cover with water in a sauce-pan and boil until tender.
2. Brown pork over medium-high heat in a 3-quart pot. Drain off fat. Add onions, green onions, parsley, and garlic. Cook on medium heat 10 minutes, stirring constantly.
3. Mix in carrots. Using a fork, mash some of the carrots but keep the dish lumpy. Season with salt and black pepper. Serve warm.

Pickled Carrots

Makes 2 pints

This is an easy-to-make, calorie-wise snack. Pickled carrots are especially good in cold Bloody Marys.

16 fresh, tender young carrots
2 sterilized pint jars with lids
2 cloves garlic, thinly sliced
½ teaspoon dill seed

¼ teaspoon celery seed
3 cups water
⅔ cup vinegar
3 tablespoons salt

1. Peel and cut carrots into 3- or 4-inch sticks. Rinse and drain. Pack into 2 sterile pint jars.
2. Add garlic, dill seed, and celery seed.
3. Bring water, vinegar, and salt to a boil in a 3-quart pot. Pour over carrot sticks. Cover with sterilized lids and refrigerate. Let stand overnight before using. Keeps in the refrigerator indefinitely.

Maque Choux (Stewed Corn)

Makes 10 servings

This dish usually showed up on our supper table during the summer, when corn was plentiful. It can be made into a main dish by adding shrimp. Our area's original inhabitants were the Taensa and Ouachita peoples. These Native Americans introduced Louisiana colonists to corn.

10 ears corn, shucked, or 2 (15-ounce) cans whole-kernel corn, drained
½ cup vegetable oil, butter, or bacon grease
1 large tomato, chopped
1 medium bell pepper, chopped

1 cup chopped onion
½ cup chopped celery
3 cloves garlic, finely minced
Salt and ground black pepper
½ pound small shrimp, peeled and deveined (optional)

1. Rinse corn and scrape kernels from the cobs. Heat oil in a skillet over medium-high heat and add corn. Cook 5 minutes, stirring constantly.
2. Add remaining ingredients, except shrimp. Cook on low heat until onions are transparent, about 20 minutes, stirring frequently.
3. Add shrimp and cook until they turn pink, about 5 minutes. Adjust seasoning and serve hot.

Easy Corn Pudding

Makes 8 servings

Growing up, we loved fresh corn from the field, and we'd douse boiled corn on the cob with lots of butter and sprinkle it with salt. This, however, is a modern dish that takes advantage of convenience products. It has become one of my family's favorites.

8 tablespoons (1 stick) butter
1 box (8.5 ounces) corn muffin mix
1 (16-ounce) can corn, with liquid, or 1 can creamed corn

8 ounces sour cream
1 large egg

1. Preheat oven to 350°F. Melt butter in a 1-quart microwave-safe bowl. Add remaining ingredients and mix well.
2. Pour into a buttered 8×8-inch casserole dish. Bake until mixture is set, approximately 45 minutes.

Shrimp-Stuffed Eggplant

Makes 8 servings

Many residents of the German Coast prided themselves in swimming in and sometimes across the Mississippi River, my grandfather Ulysses Tregre among them. That waterway provided not only amusement and exercise but also an abundance of food. River shrimp is a delicacy almost unknown now, but before large supermarkets started popping up, river shrimp was one of the few fish protein sources available to the people who lived along the river. No taste is as sublime as the delicate flavor of river shrimp cooked with butter beans, okra, squash, or eggplant. Our vegetables were fresh from a garden fertilized with the natural waste that came from the animals that lived in the yard. Eggplant was just one of the delicious gifts from my dad's garden; we did not have to buy any fresh vegetables. Even though my immediate family made this dish with river shrimp, others stuffed eggplant with ground beef or ham. My aunt Gertrude used finely chopped chicken.

4 medium eggplants
1 tablespoon butter, plus ¼ cup
    butter, melted
1 pound shrimp, coarsely chopped,
    or ground beef or chopped ham
¾ cup chopped onion

¼ cup chopped celery
2 cloves garlic, minced
2 cups crushed crackers or French
    bread crumbs, divided
1 large egg
Salt and black pepper to taste

1. Preheat oven to 350°F. Cut eggplants in half horizontally. Oil cut sides. Place face down on a rimmed cookie sheet and bake until tender, about 15 minutes. Scoop out pulp and set aside, discarding big clumps of seeds. Set shells aside.
2. Melt 1 tablespoon butter in a large skillet over medium heat and cook shrimp until just pink, about 4 minutes. Add eggplant pulp, onion, celery, and garlic. Cook 10 minutes, stirring constantly. Stir in 1 cup cracker crumbs. Add egg and mix well.
3. Spoon filling into eggplant shells. Mix remaining cup cracker crumbs with ¼ cup melted butter. Top eggplant halves with buttered crumbs. Bake until golden brown, about 20–30 minutes. Serve warm.

Creole Eggplant Casserole

Makes 6 servings

1 large eggplant, peeled and cut into
    ½-inch slices
1 large onion, thinly sliced
1 green bell pepper, sliced

2 tomatoes, thinly sliced
Salt and ground black pepper
1 pound cheddar cheese, grated
1 (5.5-ounce) can tomato or V-8 juice

1. Preheat oven to 350°F. Grease the bottom and sides of an 8×8-inch baking dish. Lightly season prepared vegetables with salt and pepper. Layer vegetables and cheese until all is used up, ending with cheese.
2. Pour tomato juice over everything. Bake until vegetables are tender, 35–45 minutes. Serve warm.

Fried Eggplant with Sugar

Makes 4 servings

This is an unusual side dish that many folks in our area enjoy. I wonder if the sugar became a part of the recipe before cooks realized that the bitterness sometimes found in eggplants can be removed with a salt soak and a rinse in cold water. Or maybe sugar eggplant is popular because Galatoire's, the famous restaurant in the New Orleans French Quarter, serves a similar dish.

1 medium eggplant
1 teaspoon salt
Vegetable oil for frying
2 large eggs

½ cup water
¼ teaspoon salt
1½ cups cornmeal or corn flour
¼ cup granulated sugar

1. Wash unpeeled eggplant and cut into ½ inch rounds. Sprinkle with salt and set aside for 30 minutes. Rinse in cold water. Pat dry.
2. Heat 1 inch oil in a deep skillet or fryer until it reaches 350°F. Mix eggs with water and salt. Dip eggplant into egg wash, then into cornmeal, then back into egg wash, and back into cornmeal.
3. Fry in hot oil. Drain and sprinkle lightly with sugar. Serve warm.

Shrimp and Crab Stuffed Mirliton

Makes 12 servings

This dish is traditionally served along with turkey and all the trimmings at Thanksgiving. It is also filling enough to serve as a main dish.

6 large mirlitons
Water for boiling
1 cup (2 sticks) butter, divided
2 cups chopped onion
1 cup chopped celery
6 cloves garlic, mashed
⅓ cup chopped parsley
2 teaspoons salt
½ teaspoon dried thyme
½ teaspoon ground black pepper

½ teaspoon salt-based liquid crab boil (from specialty stores or online)
¼ teaspoon powdered bay leaf or dried oregano
2 pounds medium shrimp, shelled and deveined
1 pound lump crabmeat
4 cups fresh bread crumbs, divided

1. Preheat oven to 350°F. Cut mirlitons in half lengthwise. Place in a large pot and cover with water. Boil until tender, 45–60 minutes. Remove seeds and discard. Using a scoop or soup spoon, carefully remove pulp, being careful not to break the shell. Chop pulp. Set both pulp and shell aside.
2. Melt 1 stick butter in a 3-quart skillet. Add onion, celery, garlic, parsley, salt, thyme, pepper, crab boil, and bay leaf. Stir well. Cook on medium-high heat until onion turns translucent. Add mirliton pulp, shrimp, and crabmeat. Cook until shrimp turns pink, about 3 minutes. Stir in 2 cups bread crumbs.
3. Mound mixture into reserved mirliton shells. Melt remaining stick butter and combine well with remaining 2 cups bread crumbs. Sprinkle buttered crumbs on top of stuffed mirlitons. Bake until lightly browned and heated through, about 30 minutes. Serve warm.

Roasted Okra

Makes 5 pounds

This basic recipe makes a large amount that can easily be portioned and frozen.

5 pounds small, fresh okra, trimmed
   and sliced
⅓ cup vegetable oil

1 large onion, finely chopped
1 (8-ounce) can tomato sauce

1. Preheat oven to 350°F. Mix all ingredients and place in an even layer on a rimmed baking sheet. Roast, stirring every 20 minutes, until okra is tender and starting to brown, about 45 minutes to 1 hour depending on size of okra.
2. Cool completely and place in 1-quart freezer-safe bags for freezing.

Smothered Okra and Shrimp

Makes 4–6 servings

Smoked sausage adds a lot of flavor and can be used in place of shrimp. Cook this dish without the shrimp or sausage and you have a delicious vegetarian side.

2 tablespoons vegetable oil
1 pound fresh okra, sliced
1 cup chopped onion
½ cup chopped bell pepper
½ cup chopped or crushed tomatoes

½ pound raw shrimp, chopped
   (optional)
Salt and pepper to taste
Hot cooked rice for serving

1. Heat oil in a large skillet set over medium-high heat. Cook okra, onion, and bell pepper until onions are translucent, about 5 minutes.
2. Add tomatoes. Lower heat and cook, stirring occasionally, until okra is tender but not "ropey," about 15 minutes. Add shrimp and continue cooking until shrimp turn pink, about 5 minutes. Season with salt and pepper. Serve with rice.

Okra Salad

Makes 4 servings

When I was a child, okra was one of my family's favorite vegetables. In the middle of the hot summer, my dad used his cane knife to cut the okra pods off their high stalks. We often boiled whole tender young okra and turned them into salads. This was the time before you could buy pickled okra in a jar. My dad insisted that our salads be made with olive oil, not the less expensive cooking oil. My dad's and my *pépère*'s affinity for olive oil was probably a carry-over from their German and French heritages.

16 (3–4-inch) okra pods
⅓ cup olive oil

¼ cup vinegar
Salt and pepper to taste

1. Place okra in a 3-quart pot. Cover with water and bring to a boil. Cook until okra turns bright green and is tender crisp, about 3–4 minutes.
2. Drain and place in a small serving dish. Mix together oil, vinegar, salt, and pepper. Pour over okra. Serve warm or at room temperature.

Pickled Okra

Makes 2 pints

1 pound small okra
2 sterile pint canning jars, with lids
   and screw tops
2 cloves garlic, minced
1 dried hot red pepper pod, crumbled

6 whole peppercorns
½ teaspoon celery seed
2 cups vinegar
½ cup water
3 tablespoons salt

1. Wash okra and place in pint jars, with okra tips up. Add garlic, red pepper, peppercorns, and celery seed.
2. Bring vinegar, water, and salt to a boil. Pour over okra. Cover with sterilized lids. Keeps indefinitely in refrigerator.

Caramelized Onions

Makes 2 cups

I don't know if there's anything that smells as good as onions frying in olive oil. I like to keep some in the fridge to pop on top of steak and pork chops. For pork chops, I like to mix the onions with any fruit jam.

4 tablespoons olive oil   2 large onions, sliced

Heat oil in a large skillet set over medium heat. Add onions and stir to coat. Continue cooking, stirring occasionally, until onions are caramelized to a medium-brown color, about 15 minutes. Serve immediately or store in a covered container in the refrigerator.

Creamed Spinach

Makes 6 servings

This is one of my favorite ways to cook spinach, and it makes a great side dish or a dip.

1 (10-ounce) box frozen chopped   1 (13.75-ounce) can artichoke hearts
    spinach   ¼ cup Parmesan cheese, grated
2 slices bacon, chopped   ¼ teaspoon freshly grated nutmeg
½ cup chopped onion   Salt and ground black pepper to taste
2 tablespoons all-purpose flour   Hot sauce to taste
1 cup whole milk or half-and-half

1. Cook spinach per package directions. Squeeze out water and set aside.
2. Fry bacon in a skillet until crisp. Remove from pan and set aside. Add onion to bacon grease in pan and fry over medium-high heat until medium brown, about 3 minutes. Add flour and stir well. Whisk milk into the onion mixture. Cook on medium heat, whisking constantly, until thickened.
3. Gently stir in spinach and artichoke hearts. Stir in remaining ingredients and bring to a simmer. Stir well and cook 5 minutes longer. Remove from heat. Serve hot as a side dish or as a hot dip.

Ham-Stuffed Patty Pan Squash

Makes 6 servings

Everyone on the German Coast had a garden in their backyard or on the levee, where cows grazed all day. After a hard day's work, everyone tended their gardens and took the cows home for the night. Patty pan squash is not as well known as the other squashes grown in the area, but it was always one of my favorites. This heirloom vegetable is white, flattish, and round with scalloped edges. When stuffed, it makes a beautiful presentation.

3 medium patty pan squash	1 clove garlic, minced
4 tablespoons butter, divided	1 pound ham, coarsely chopped
½ cup chopped onion	6 slices stale white bread
½ cup chopped celery	1 large egg
2 green onions, chopped	Salt and ground black pepper to taste

1. Preheat oven to 350°F. Split squash in half horizontally. Place in 5-quart pot and cover with water. Bring to a boil. Cook until fork tender. Remove from pot and drain. Remove seeds and discard. Scoop pulp from shell, being careful not to cut into shell. Reserve both pulp and shells. Mash pulp with fork.
2. Melt 2 tablespoons butter in a large skillet set over medium heat. Sauté onion, celery, green onions, and garlic 10 minutes. Add squash pulp and ham. Cook 10 minutes, stirring constantly.
3. Process bread in a food processor to make crumbs. Add half of bread crumbs and egg to squash mixture and mix well. Add salt and pepper to taste. Spoon into shells.
4. Melt remaining 2 tablespoons butter and mix with remaining bread crumbs. Top squash halves with buttered bread crumbs. Bake until tops are brown, about 22–25 minutes. Serve warm.

Summer Squash with Bacon and Onions

Makes 6 servings

All types of squash grow in south Louisiana. The yellow crookneck squash so plentiful here in the summer is one of my favorites.

2 slices bacon, chopped

½ cup chopped onion

2 tablespoons water

6 medium yellow crookneck squash, sliced or diced

Salt and ground black pepper to taste

1. Add bacon to a large skillet. Fry on medium heat until crisp. Add onion to pan and cook 3 minutes.
2. Add water and stir up the bits from the bottom of pan. Add squash. Cover and cook over medium heat until squash is tender, about 10 minutes. Season with salt and pepper. Serve hot.

Three generations of fine cooks: Mémère, Mam Papaul, and Lelia.

Roasted Sweet Potatoes with Pecan-Orange Topping

Makes 6 servings

My mom, grandmother, and great-grandmother all loved sweet potatoes. Like most gardeners, my dad planted what his family would eat, so he planted sweet potatoes. Sometimes we helped him dig them up in late summer and early fall. Before mom cooked them, my dad aged them in the dark in the backyard shed a few weeks.

1½ pounds sweet potatoes (about 3 medium potatoes)
2 green onions, thinly sliced
⅓ cup olive oil, divided

1 teaspoon salt
¼ teaspoon ground black pepper
1 tablespoon brown sugar

Topping

⅓ cup coarsely chopped pecans
2 tablespoons chopped parsley
1 tablespoon brown sugar
1 tablespoon freshly grated orange or satsuma peel

½ teaspoon cumin or toasted and crushed coriander seeds
¼ teaspoon salt
Parsley sprigs and maraschino cherries for garnish

1. Preheat oven to 400°F. Peel potatoes and cut into 1-inch cubes. Grease the bottom of a rimmed baking pan with 2 tablespoons olive oil. Place potatoes and green onions in a single layer in pan and drizzle with remaining olive oil. Sprinkle potatoes with salt, pepper, and brown sugar. Stir to evenly coat the sweet potatoes. Bake until potatoes are fork-tender, about 30 minutes.
2. To make topping, preheat oven to 325°F and bake pecans 10 minutes. Mix pecans with the remaining topping ingredients. Gently combine topping with the sweet potatoes on the baking sheet, being careful not to mash the potatoes. Place in a serving bowl and garnish with parsley sprigs. Serve warm.

Sweet Potato Croquettes

Makes 6 servings

We loved sweet potatoes prepared a variety of ways, and this was a favorite.

3 cups mashed sweet potatoes
 (2 [1-pound, 1-ounce] cans yield
 3 cups)

¾ cup chopped ham
1 cup plain bread crumbs
Butter or vegetable oil for frying

1. Divide sweet potatoes into 6 equal portions. Divide ham into 6 equal portions, about 2 tablespoons each.
2. Place a portion of sweet potato in the palm of your hand. Make a well in the center and place a portion of ham into the well. Mold the sweet potato around the ham to make a ball. Flatten slightly and form into a patty. Do same for remaining portions.
3. Coat patties with bread crumbs, making sure all surfaces are covered. Fry in a hot skillet in ¼-inch butter or oil until golden brown, or bake at 350°F for 20 minutes. Serve hot.

Baked Sweet Potatoes

Makes 8 servings

We enjoyed baked sweet potatoes with pork dinners. We always topped them with butter and sometimes with cinnamon and sugar.

8 medium sweet potatoes

½ cup (1 stick) butter

1. Preheat oven to 375°F. Wash potatoes and pat dry. Prick tops all over with a fork.
2. Lay potatoes on a cookie sheet covered with foil to catch drips. Bake until tender, approximately 45–60 minutes or more, depending on the size and age of the potatoes. Split hot potatoes open and top each with a big pat of butter and serve.

Mashed Irish Potatoes

Makes 6 servings

We called them Irish potatoes, those potatoes with the brown skin that mash so well. Did the Irish bring them over? I don't know. What I do know is that they are well loved in this area.

2 pounds Irish (white) potatoes
1½ cups half-and-half
½ cup (1 stick) butter

½ cup sour cream (optional)
½ teaspoon salt
½ teaspoon ground black pepper

1. Peel and cut potatoes into quarters. Place in a 4-quart pot, cover with water, and boil until tender, 15–20 minutes. Drain and mash potatoes.
2. Add remaining ingredients. Stir well. Adjust seasoning to taste. For guaranteed lump-free potatoes, press cooked potatoes through a ricer.

Yellow Rice

Makes 4 servings

This was a good way to use leftover rice and stretch eggs when the chickens weren't laying. This was a breakfast favorite and was typically served with a cup of hot café au lait.

2 tablespoons butter
2 cups cooked rice

2 eggs
Salt and ground black pepper to taste

1. Melt butter in a large skillet set over medium heat. Add rice and stir until grains are separated.
2. Add eggs and mix well. Cook and stir until egg is dry. Add salt and pepper to taste. Serve hot.

Polenta with Olives, Red Bell Peppers, and Basil

Makes 8 servings

Polenta is an Italian dish made with yellow grits. Grits and eggs was one of our favorite meals, so this colorful dish caught my eye and my palate. This makes an impressive cold appetizer, or a hot side dish to accompany pork or chicken. I developed this dish after trying something similar at the Biltmore estate in Asheville, North Carolina.

1 fire-roasted red bell pepper from a jar
1 ounce fresh basil leaves, roughly chopped
1 tablespoon olive oil
½ cup Kalamata olives
6 cups water
1 teaspoon ground white pepper
1 teaspoon salt
1½ cups half-and-half
¾ cup butter
2 cups uncooked polenta
1½ cups plus 2 tablespoons grated Parmesan cheese
Fresh basil leaves for garnish

1. Rinse the bell pepper and pat dry. Place in a blender and puree. Set aside. Puree basil with olive oil. Set aside. Puree olives. Set aside.
2. Bring water, white pepper, and salt to a boil in a 5-quart saucepan set over medium-high heat. Stir in half-and-half and butter. Gently stir in polenta. Reduce heat and cook 25 minutes, stirring often. Stir in 1½ cups Parmesan cheese.
3. Divide polenta equally among 3 medium mixing bowls. Add bell pepper puree to one bowl of polenta, pureed basil mixture to another bowl, and olive puree to the last bowl. Stir each well.
4. Line the inside of an 8-inch round cake pan with plastic wrap. Spread the contents of one polenta bowl into pan and top with plastic wrap. Spread the contents of another polenta bowl on top of first layer and top again with plastic wrap. Repeat process with remaining bowl. Refrigerate until firm, about 1 hour.
5. Remove the first two layers of polenta and the layer of plastic wrap on the bottom layer. Grasp the edges of the plastic wrap to flip one of the removed layers on top of bottom layer in the pan. Discard plastic and repeat process with remaining layer. You should have a three-colored stack. Press polenta layers in place. Turn out on a serving dish. Sprinkle with 2 tablespoons Parmesan cheese and garnish with basil leaves. Chill and cut into wedges to serve. To serve hot, heat in a microwave oven 5 minutes or longer, depending on the wattage of your oven.

Riz Au Fiev (Rice with Peas)

Makes 6 servings

Some people call this dish jambalaya, while others call it hoppin' John. On the German Coast it was called by its French name, *riz au fiev* (pronounced re au fiev). Really, it's just rice cooked with black-eyed or field peas.

1½ cups fresh or frozen black-eyed peas or field peas
6 ounces pickle meat (pickled pork), boiled until just tender and diced
6 cups water
1 tablespoon vegetable oil

1 cup raw rice, rinsed and drained
½ cup chopped onion
1 tablespoon chopped bell pepper
¾ teaspoon salt
¼ teaspoon ground black pepper

1. Boil peas and meat in water until peas are tender, about 45 minutes. Skim and discard foam. Drain and reserve water.
2. Heat oil in a large skillet set over medium-high heat and stir-fry rice until it turns light brown. Add peas, meat, onion, bell pepper, salt, pepper, and 2 cups reserved water. Bring to a boil, cover, lower heat, and cook until rice is tender, about 20 minutes. Serve warm.

Tomato Mayonnaise Sandwiches
Makes 4 servings

When I was in school, this was a favorite afternoon snack. I didn't know that anyone else thought these sandwiches were something special until my daughter married a man from Mississippi and these were served as open-faced sandwiches at her wedding shower.

8 slices white bread
½ cup mayonnaise

2 large tomatoes
Salt and ground black pepper

1. Lay the bread out on a clean cloth. Spread mayonnaise on one side of each slice.
2. Cut each tomato into 4 slices. Place one tomato slice on each bread slice spread with mayonnaise. Sprinkle lightly with salt and black pepper. Close to make 4 sandwiches. Trim crusts. Cover with a damp paper towel until ready to serve.

Creole Mac and Cheese
Makes 12 servings

Okay, this isn't a vegetable, but it's a fantastic side. It's no ordinary mac and cheese because of the addition of milk and eggs, which make it custardy and rich. This dish has been a family favorite for generations.

3 quarts water (for boiling pasta)
5 teaspoons salt, divided
1 pound spaghetti or elbow macaroni
2 (10-ounce) cans evaporated milk
1 cup water

4 large eggs, slightly beaten
4 tablespoons (½ stick) butter, melted
¼ teaspoon ground black pepper
2 cups shredded Cheddar cheese

1. Preheat oven to 350°F. Bring water and 4 teaspoons salt to a boil. Add pasta and boil until just tender. Place drained pasta in a buttered 9×13-inch casserole dish.
2. Blend together milk, water, eggs, remaining 1 teaspoon salt, butter, and pepper. Mix well. Pour over pasta and top with cheese.
3. Bake until custard is set and cheese is melted, about 35–40 minutes. Serve warm.

Quick Brown Roux–Based Crawfish Bisque
page 8

Andouille
page 23

Cochon de Lait, ready to serve
page 32

Converted Rice Jambalaya for a Crowd
page 34

German Coast Chicken Stew
page 61

Shrimp Remoulade
page 75

Crawfish Pasta
page 86

Fried Soft-Shell Crab
page 91

Butter Beans with Shrimp
page 109

New Year's Day Black-Eyed Peas
page 110

Shrimp and Crab Stuffed Mirliton
page 121

Roasted Okra
page 122

Roasted Sweet Potatoes with Pecan-Orange Topping
page 127

Cracklin Cornbread
page 139

Biscuits Feuillete
page 141

Banana Bread
page 142

Gingerbread Cake
page 165

Divinity Angel Roll
page 163

Easter Eggs
page 69

Bread Pudding with Meringue
page 167

Tarte à la Bouille
page 168

Pecan Pie
page 172

Chocolate Cream Puffs and Cream Puff Swans
pages 186–187

St. Joseph Altar, with baked breads, cookies, and other foods
pages 183–184

BREADS

JUST LIKE RICE, bread was a staple on German Coast tables. It was inexpensive to make, and the ingredients were easy to come by. In early days, the leaven used was made with mashed potatoes or a piece of bread from a previous batch of dough mixed with water and left to the elements to ferment. It's hard for us to imagine, but there was no baking powder until the late 1800s. But they did have bicarbonate of soda and a variety of acids that could be used to activate the soda to produce gas to leaven quick breads.

I have always loved making yeast-raised breads. What could be better than the aroma of baking bread wafting through the house? Biscuits, cornbread, yeast rolls, and monkey bread were family favorites. My mom told me that Mémère and MomMom (Mam Papaul) made bread with a homemade starter.

I have a daughter who is a pastry chef, and she makes the most delicious breads I have ever tasted. Her interest in this field began when she helped me in the kitchen as I made homemade breads for holidays. She has developed a sourdough recipe for people who are gluten sensitive. Maybe one day she will share that recipe with me, as well as her recipes for macaroons and rolled meringue.

Old-Fashioned Potato Rolls

Makes 4 large loaves or 4 dozen rolls

In college, how I envied my friend Ginny, who scheduled a class in experimental foods at the University of Southwestern Louisiana. She developed this potato bread recipe that is similar to what my mom remembers my grandmother making. Here is an updated version of Ginny Ballay Smith's recipe.

2 medium red potatoes	2 teaspoons salt
5 cups all-purpose flour, sifted	1½ cups very warm water, 115°F
⅔ cup sugar	4 large eggs
4 teaspoons quick-rise yeast	½ cup (1 stick) butter, softened

1. Peel potatoes and boil until tender. Put them through a ricer and measure out 1 cup. Set aside.
2. Place flour, sugar, yeast, and salt in a large mixing bowl. Combine well, using a wire whisk or spoon.
3. Add warm water to flour mixture. Using the paddle attachment of a heavy-duty mixer, beat on low speed for 3 minutes. Add potatoes and beat well.
4. Add eggs one at a time, beating well after each addition. Beat in butter. Using the dough hook, knead dough until it pulls from the side of the bowl, about 3 minutes.
5. Roll dough into a ball and put in a greased bowl. Cover with greased plastic wrap, set in a warm place, and let rise until double in bulk, about 1 hour. Punch dough down, cover with plastic wrap, and refrigerate 24 hours. From this point, dough will keep in refrigerator for a week. If dough rises in the refrigerator, punch down.
6. Remove dough from refrigerator 2 hours before forming into rolls and baking. To form rolls, dump dough onto a hard, floured surface. Knead lightly. If making rolls, divide dough into four, then each piece into twelve. Roll each piece into a ball and place into 4 greased 9×13-inch baking pans or muffin tins. Cover lightly with a dish towel and let rise until doubled, about one hour. For loaves, divide dough into four, shape each piece into a loaf, and place each loaf into an oiled loaf pan.
7. A half hour before ready to bake, preheat oven to 375°F. Bake until deep brown, about 20 minutes. Serve warm.

Freezing unbaked rolls: After forming rolls, freeze on a tray. When rolls are frozen, place in a plastic bag and return to the freezer for up to 1 month.

Baking frozen rolls: Remove rolls from plastic bag. Place on a well-greased pan to thaw. Let rise until double in bulk. A half hour before baking, preheat oven to 375°F and bake until golden brown, about 20 minutes.

Dinner Rolls

Makes 18 dinner rolls

In addition to dinner rolls, this recipe makes a very good monkey bread (*recipe follows*).

1 cup lukewarm milk
1 (¼-ounce) package yeast
½ cup (1 stick) butter, slightly
   softened

2 large eggs
¼ cup sugar
1 teaspoon salt
4½ cups all-purpose flour, divided

1. Place milk and yeast in a large mixing bowl. Let stand 5 minutes. Stir well.
2. Add butter, eggs, sugar, salt, and 1 cup flour. Beat by hand until everything is mixed well, or use a paddle on a heavy-duty mixer at medium speed.
3. Add remaining flour and mix to make a soft dough. Beat until smooth. Using the dough hook of a standing mixer, knead at medium speed until dough pulls from the side of the bowl, about 5 minutes. Cover with a damp cloth and let rise until dough is double in bulk.
4. Preheat oven to 375°F and grease 18 muffin tins. Punch dough down. Form dough balls about half the size of an egg. Place two balls into each prepared muffin cup. Let rise until double in size, about 30–45 minutes. Bake rolls until lightly browned, about 15 minutes.

Pecan Monkey Bread

2 sticks butter
1 cup white sugar
1 cup brown sugar
1 cup chopped pecans

2 teaspoons cinnamon
Fresh dough balls from Dinner Rolls
   recipe (*above*)

Melt butter. Blend together sugars, pecans, and cinnamon. Roll dough balls in butter, then in sugar-pecan mixture. Place in well-buttered loaf pan. Let rise until double in bulk. Bake at 375°F until lightly browned, about 30 minutes.

Bacon Buns
Makes 12 rolls

I based this recipe on the fantastic bacon bread at Paul Bocuse's Monsieur Paul Restaurant at Walt Disney World in Florida. I like serving them with butter and a cup of café au lait.

2½ cups bread flour
2 tablespoons sugar
1 (¼-ounce) packet quick-rise yeast, or 2¼ teaspoons loose yeast
½ teaspoon salt

1 cup very warm water (120°F)
½ cup bacon fat
3 slices bacon, crisply fried and crumbled

1. Mix flour, sugar, yeast, and salt in the bowl of a standing mixer. Attach bowl to mixer and put paddle in place.
2. In a separate bowl, combine warm water and bacon fat. Add bacon-fat mixture and crumbled bacon to flour mixture and beat on medium speed 2 minutes. Change to dough hook and knead at medium speed until dough pulls away from the sides of the bowl, about 3 minutes. Cover with plastic wrap and let dough rest 10 minutes.
3. Lightly grease a 12-serving muffin tin with vegetable oil. Turn dough onto a lightly floured hard surface. Cut into 2 equal pieces. Roll each piece into a log 2½ inches in diameter. Cut each log into 6 equal pieces. Shape into balls and place each ball in a prepared muffin cup. Let rise in a warm place (80–90°F) until doubled in bulk, about 30 minutes.
4. Twenty minutes before dough has risen, preheat oven to 375°F. When dough has risen, bake until nicely browned, about 25 minutes. Buns will be crisp on the outside and soft on the inside.

Brioche
Makes 1 large or 2 small brioche

In addition to the traditional French breakfast bread called brioche, this sweet bread dough can be used to make cinnamon rolls. Mam Papaul and my mom liked to top their brioche with cooked coconut, but jams, jellies, and marmalades are also good. This bread freezes and reheats well.

½ cup lukewarm milk

1 (¼-ounce) package yeast

½ cup (1 stick) butter, softened

2 large eggs

¼ cup sugar, plus additional for sprinkling

½ teaspoon crushed anise seeds or other flavoring, such as vanilla

¼ teaspoon salt

2½ cups all-purpose flour, divided

1. Place milk and yeast in a large mixing bowl. Stir well and let stand 5 minutes.
2. Stir in butter, eggs, ¼ cup sugar, anise, and salt. Add 1 cup flour. Beat well by hand until flour is moistened, or use a paddle on a heavy-duty mixer.
3. Add enough of the remaining flour to make a soft, sticky dough. Beat until smooth, 5 minutes by hand, or at medium speed using the dough hook of a standing mixer. Cover with a damp cloth and let rise in a warm place until dough has doubled in bulk, about an hour. Punch down, cover, and let rise again for 1 hour.
4. Heat oven to 375°F. Punch dough down and knead lightly to form a smooth ball. (If dough is a little hard to handle, place in the refrigerator for an hour. Do not add more flour.)
5. Reserve a piece of dough the size of an egg. Place remainder of dough in a buttered brioche mold, or in a 2- or 3-quart ovenproof bowl with straight sides. Make an indentation in the center of the top of the dough and place the dough egg in the indentation. Butter top of dough and sprinkle with sugar.
6. Cover and let rise until double in size. Bake approximately 45 minutes or until browned and internal temperature is 180°F. Serve warm or at room temperature.

Compound Butters for Bread

Cane Syrup Butter: Blend 2 tablespoons cane syrup with 1 stick butter and 2 tablespoons chopped toasted pecans.

Fruit Butter: Blend 2 tablespoons any fruit preserve with 1 stick butter.

Savory Butter: Blend ¼ teaspoon garlic powder and ½ teaspoon onion powder with 1 stick butter and 4 ounces cream cheese.

Cinnamon Butter: Blend 1 stick butter with 3 tablespoons brown sugar and ¼ teaspoon cinnamon.

*The bread man delivered bread to our house each day.
He sold only two kinds of bread: short bread, meaning sliced bread,
and long bread, meaning French bread. We children all wanted the croston,
which is what we called the end of a loaf of French bread. We'd fill it
with cane syrup, and it made a great snack. When my mom,
Lelia, was growing up, the bread man delivered his
goods in a horse-drawn carriage.*

Gourgues Bakery bread wagon

Pain Perdu

Makes 4 servings

My mom says that when she was a schoolgirl, there was a neighborhood bakery just a few doors away from the house I live in now. The baker, Mr. Gourgues, was a relative. Later, when I was going to grade school and the bread man delivered a loaf of sliced white bread to our door every morning, anything not eaten the same day was considered stale. We were a thrifty family, and we used our stale bread to make bread pudding and *pain perdu*, now commonly known as French toast. *Pain perdu* is just a fancy name for bread dipped in a wash of sugar, cinnamon, nutmeg, eggs, and milk, and fried in butter to a beautiful brown. We often served it for breakfast with cane syrup, fresh strawberry preserves, or blackberry jelly, along with café au lait. *Pain perdu* is one of the first things I learned to make.

1 cup whole milk	Pinch salt
1 large egg	4 slices stale bread
1 tablespoon sugar	4 tablespoons butter
¼ teaspoon cinnamon	Cooked bacon, jelly, preserves, or
¼ teaspoon freshly grated nutmeg	cane syrup for serving

1. In a shallow soup bowl, whisk together milk, egg, sugar, cinnamon, nutmeg, and salt. Dip each slice of bread into mixture, covering both sides.
2. Melt butter in a skillet set over medium heat. Add dipped bread slices to butter and cook until browned, about 2–3 minutes per side. Serve with bacon, jelly, preserves, or cane syrup.

Cracklin Cornbread

Makes 6 servings

We only had cracklins after a boucherie. Sometimes we ate them all before my mom had a chance to make cornbread. When she did make cracklin cornbread, we ate it with fried ham or bacon, fried eggs, and a cup of café au lait before hurrying off to school.

1 cup yellow cornmeal	1 cup whole milk
1 cup all-purpose flour	½ cup (1 stick) butter, melted
2 tablespoons sugar	1 large egg
4 teaspoons baking powder	½ cup cracklins, cut into small pieces
½ teaspoon salt	

1. Preheat oven to 400°F. Grease an 8×8-inch baking pan, or an 8-inch cast-iron skillet. In a large bowl, sift together cornmeal, flour, sugar, baking powder, and salt.
2. Lightly beat milk, butter, and egg together. Add to flour mixture. Gently mix until well blended.
3. Mix in cracklins. Bake until lightly browned, about 25 minutes. Serve warm.

Galettes

Makes 4 servings

These fried rectangles of dough are reminiscent of Mexican sopapillas, New Orleans–style beignets, Acadian *gollyettes*, and Spanish *galletas*. The Germans and Indians also have their versions of "fry" bread. Mémère often came across the backyard to our house to cook galettes for us on cold winter mornings. She traditionally put a slit in the center of the dough just before dropping them into the hot oil. If they're not slit, they puff up like French beignets. Galettes are delicious served with cane syrup, fresh fig preserves, or powdered sugar.

2 cups all-purpose flour
4 teaspoons baking powder
½ teaspoon salt
⅔ cup cold water, or more

Vegetable oil for frying
Syrup, jam, or powdered sugar for
serving

1. In a medium bowl, sift together flour, baking powder, and salt. (Or use 2 cups self-rising flour.) Add enough water to make a soft, sticky dough.
2. Roll out into a very thin rectangle, about ⅛-inch thick. Cut into 2×3-inch rectangles with a floured knife. Make a 2-inch slit in the center of each if you do not want them to puff up.
3. Heat 1 inch oil in a deep skillet to 350°F. Drop galettes into hot oil, frying only 3 or 4 at a time. Turn to brown both sides. Serve hot with your favorite syrup or jam, or powdered sugar.

Banana Fritters

Makes 6 servings

Mama often served fried plantains as a side dish for supper, but she'd make these crispy banana fritters for breakfast.

Vegetable oil for frying
2¼ cups all-purpose flour, divided
½ cup whole milk
1 large egg
1 teaspoon sugar

½ teaspoon salt
5 small bananas, cut into 2-inch
chunks
Powdered sugar for dusting

1. In a large skillet or fryer set on medium-high heat, preheat 1 inch oil to 360°F. Place 1½ cups flour, milk, egg, sugar, and salt in a small bowl. Beat well to make batter.
2. Place remaining ¾ cup flour in a shallow bowl. Roll banana chunks in flour, dip in batter, then roll in flour again.
3. Drop into hot oil and fry on all sides until golden brown, 3–4 minutes. Dust with powdered sugar. Serve hot.

Biscuits Feuillete
(pronounced feuil-tay)
Makes 8–10 biscuits

This was Mam Papaul's special way to make flaky, buttery biscuits, a variation of the French feuillantine, a flaky French pastry rolled out and turned upon itself several times. She learned this technique from Mémère. My mother made these biscuits often, and I learned from her this long-ago carryover from that German/French heritage. At the request of my young *tante* (aunt) Una, my friends and I would spend the night at my grandmother's house, where we enjoyed these biscuits with hot cocoa in the evening, or we'd have them with "get-up coffee" in the morning. My grandmother's way of getting us up was to deliver a cup of sweetened café au lait while we were still in bed.

3 cups all-purpose flour
4 teaspoons baking powder
¼ teaspoon salt

½ cup (1 stick) cold butter
1 cup whole milk
¼ cup (½ stick) butter, melted

1. Preheat oven to 425°F. Sift together flour, baking powder, and salt. Cut cold butter into the flour mixture using a pastry blender until mixture resembles small peas. Add milk and mix lightly.
2. Flour a hard surface. Gently knead dough 12 times. Roll out to ½-inch thickness.
3. Brush half of the surface with melted butter. Fold unbasted side over basted side. Roll out again to ¼-inch thickness and brush half with melted butter. Repeat 5 times.
4. Roll dough to ½-inch thickness. Cut into 2½-inch squares with a floured knife. Bake until biscuits are lightly browned and bottoms are crisp, approximately 12 minutes. Serve hot.

Banana Bread

Makes 12 servings

I *love* bananas. For this recipe, use extremely ripe bananas for the best flavor. If they're so far gone that the skin is black, that's okay. Overripe bananas freeze well in the peel and can also be frozen mashed and portioned out for later use. In the early days of the German Coast, the tropical-looking banana tree was a common part of plantation landscapes.

1 cup sugar
½ cup (1 stick) butter, slightly
   softened
2 large eggs
1½ cups very ripe mashed bananas

1½ tablespoons lemon juice
2¼ cups all-purpose flour
3 teaspoons baking powder
½ teaspoon salt

1. Preheat oven to 350°F. Grease a 9×5×3-inch loaf pan or Bundt pan. In a large bowl, use a large spoon to cream together sugar and butter. Add eggs one at a time, beating well after each addition. Stir in bananas and lemon juice.
2. Add flour, baking powder, and salt. Beat until flour is completely absorbed into liquid. Pour into prepared pan and bake until top springs back when touched, about 1 hour. Cool in pan 5 minutes. Remove from pan and cool completely.

Cinnamon Buns

Makes 8–12 buns

1 cup lukewarm milk
1 (¼-ounce) package yeast
½ cup (1 stick) butter
2 large eggs

¼ cup sugar
1 teaspoon salt
1 teaspoon vanilla extract
4½ cups all-purpose flour, divided

Filling

½ cup sugar
½ teaspoon cinnamon

2 tablespoons butter, melted
⅓ cup raisins

Glaze

1 cup powdered sugar
½ teaspoon almond flavoring

Water

1. Preheat oven to 375°F and butter a 9×13-inch baking pan. Place milk and yeast in a mixing bowl. Let stand 5 minutes. Stir well.
2. Add butter, eggs, sugar, salt, vanilla, and 1 cup of flour. Beat by hand until well combined, or use a paddle on a heavy-duty mixer at medium speed.
3. Add remaining flour and beat until smooth. You should have a soft dough. Cover with a damp cloth and let rise until dough is double in bulk, about 1½ hours.
4. Roll dough out to a 12×17-inch rectangle. Make filling by mixing together sugar, cinnamon, and butter. Sprinkle sugar mixture and raisins over dough surface and roll up jellyroll fashion, starting on one of the long sides.
5. Using a sharp, floured knife, cut dough into 2-inch pieces and place in buttered pan. Cover with a damp cloth and let rise until double in bulk, about 1 hour. Bake until golden brown, approximately 45 minutes.
6. Make glaze by combining sugar, almond flavoring, and enough water in a small bowl to make a thin icing. Drizzle over warm buns.

*My dad always thought tins of cookies made good presents.
He used to tell us how, as a youngster, he'd been friends back in
Wallace with an African American girl named Rose, and the two
used to ride around Evergreen Plantation in a goat cart.
When his family moved, he lost contact with Rose.
Many years later, as an old woman, Rose moved to Hahnville
to live with her daughter. When my dad heard that this childhood
friend was nearby, he went for a visit, and they recalled the
good times they enjoyed as children. His gift to her,
after all those years, was a tin of cookies.*

DESSERTS, SWEETS, AND CONDIMENTS

FEW DESSERTS HERE have German origins. Most traditional desserts from Louisiana's German Coast originated with the French. Most of the sweets the women in my family cooked revolved around things that grew here, and recipes for just about all of them could be found in the pages of antique cookbooks.

We didn't have dessert every day, but we always had fresh and canned fruit in the house, along with cheese, jellies, and preserves. Our weekday suppers often ended with cheese, crackers, and some type of fruit preserve or jelly. Our jellies and preserves were homemade. With fig, satsuma, pear, and plum trees in our backyards, that was a given.

Sunday desserts were usually cakes made with butter and fresh eggs from the yard. Sometimes we took Sunday drives up the river looking for persimmons, or we trekked forty-five miles north to Ponchatoula for strawberries. Occasionally we had sweet biscuits with fresh strawberries and whipped cream, and, yes, that was breakfast. Strawberries and whipped cream on homemade sponge cake was special enough for a Sunday dessert. Cakes, jelly-rolls, cream puffs, and éclairs were also served on Sunday, as well as holidays.

Christmas was always a special time for sweets. My grandmother Mam Papaul always served gumbo and potato salad after midnight mass. She also went the extra mile and made floating island (our German Coast version of eggnog) and rocks (pecan-and-date cookies like German hermits). After Mam Papaul died, my mom continued the same Christmas gumbo and dessert tradition.

For us, crêpes with preserves or syrup was a breakfast food, not a dessert, even if we occasionally had them with ice cream. Carrot, vanilla wafer, and oatmeal cakes are among many of the area's newer generation of favored cakes. To me, "newer generation" means that they first became popular during the last sixty years.

Anything with meringue, including bread pudding, held a special place in our hearts.

With sugarcane fields and sugar refineries lining the banks of the Mississippi River, it is no wonder that candies and other goodies made with both white granulated and brown sugar abound in our repertoire of sweets.

Pecans and chocolate made gold cake a favorite. Coconut and divinity frosting brought a devil's food cake to glorious heights of deliciousness. A silver cake—a white cake flavored with almond—was the ultimate wedding cake, and it still is the favored wedding cake on the river. Common pies included pecan, coconut cream, chocolate, banana, apple, and lemon. Although pies were not her favorite thing to make, Mam Papaul made *tarte à la bouille*, a boiled custard pie, for Pépère Zoot for his birthday each year. I can still remember my mom making her first *tarte à la bouille* for my dad.

Blackberry jellyroll was a favorite Sunday dessert not only in our family but all along the German Coast. Mémère Nellie, Mam Papaul, and her daughters often raised money for Holy Rosary Church by selling jellyrolls in a variety of flavors. My parrain (godfather), Wilson Zeringue, loved to make jellyrolls. One year he made $10,000 selling jellyrolls for Holy Angels Church in Waggaman.

Interior of Our Lady of the Holy Rosary Church, Hahnville.
This church was demolished in the 1950s.

Blackberry Jellyroll

Makes 8 servings

This was my mom and Mam Papaul's specialty, and a favorite Sunday dessert Mama made with her wild blackberry jelly. When we visited Pépère Tregre and Aunt Hedwidge in Wallace, my mom always brought along a blackberry jellyroll. My dad usually picked the blackberries by the local railroad track and in the nearby woods.

4 large eggs
1 cup plus 2 tablespoons sugar
3 tablespoons water
1 teaspoon vanilla extract
1 cup cake flour

1 teaspoon baking powder
¼ teaspoon salt
1 cup blackberry jelly or your
    favorite jelly

1. Preheat oven to 400° F. Line a 10×15-inch jellyroll pan with wax or parchment paper.
2. Rinse a large mixing bowl and mixer beaters with hot water. Beat eggs using medium speed until very light, about 2 minutes. Add 1 cup sugar a little at a time and beat until dissolved, about 10 minutes. Add water and vanilla. Beat until well combined.
3. Sift flour, baking powder, and salt together. Gently fold into egg mixture until well incorporated. Spread evenly in prepared pan. Bake until lightly browned and cake springs back when touched, about 15–20 minutes.
4. Sprinkle a 20-inch cloth with 2 tablespoons sugar. Turn baked cake onto cloth. While cake is still warm, spread with a thin layer of jelly.
5. Have someone lift the cloth at the 10-inch end of the cake. Roll the cake from the cloth side as the person holding the cloth gently pulls the cloth away from you as you roll. Complete the roll and wrap in waxed paper. Cool completely before slicing. This cake does not have to be refrigerated. It will not last long enough for you to even think about storing it.

Yeast-Raised Chocolate Cake
with Orange Whipped-Cream Frosting
Makes a 4-layer, 9-inch cake

I passed my high school chemistry class because of this cake. Science was never my best subject, so when my teacher offered extra points for chemistry projects, I took him up on it. Knowing that he loved chocolate cake, I made two types, one leavened with conventional baking powder and one made from a recipe from my grandmother, which was made with yeast. My teacher chose the yeast-raised cake as the better of the two, and he later admitted he thought he was choosing the one made with baking powder. For this recipe, I brush my layers with a cake wash, a thin, flavored syrup, which makes the cake extremely moist.

3 cups plus 6 tablespoons sifted cake
    flour (sift, then measure)
1 (¼-ounce) package quick-rise yeast
1 teaspoon baking soda
½ teaspoon salt
2 cups sugar
1 cup (2 sticks) butter, softened
3 large eggs
1¼ cups whole milk

4 ounces semisweet chocolate,
    melted
½ cup coarsely chopped pecans
1 teaspoon vanilla extract
Orange-Flavored Cake Wash
    (*recipe follows*)
Whipped-Cream Frosting
    (*recipe follows*)
1 teaspoon grated orange rind

1. Line bottoms of two 9-inch round cake pans with parchment or waxed paper. Grease and flour sides of pans. Sift together cake flour, yeast, baking soda, and salt. Set aside.
2. Use an electric mixer at medium speed to cream sugar with butter until light and fluffy, about 3 minutes. Add eggs one at a time, beating 1 minute after each addition.
3. Warm milk to 115°F. Add chocolate to milk. Add flour mixture to butter mixture alternately with milk mixture. Beat on medium speed 5 minutes. Stir in pecans and vanilla.
4. Divide batter evenly between the 2 prepared pans. Let rise in a warm place to ¾ depth of the pans, about 2 hours.
5. About 20 minutes before ready to bake, preheat oven to 350°F. Bake layers until a toothpick inserted in the center of cakes comes out clean, about 45 minutes. (You can also place filled pans in the refrigerator for 6 hours and then bake, which should take about 1 hour.) When layers are done, cool in

pans 5 minutes. Invert onto racks and cool completely. Slice each layer in half horizontally to make 4 layers in all.

6. Brush top of each layer with Orange-Flavored Cake Wash. Fill and frost with Whipped-Cream Frosting. Garnish with grated orange rind. Refrigerate left-over cake.

Orange-Flavored Cake Wash

Makes about 1⅓ cups

1 cup sugar
½ cup water
1 tablespoon grated orange rind

3 tablespoons Grand Marnier or orange juice

In a small saucepan set over medium heat, heat sugar, water, and orange rind until sugar is melted. Remove from heat and stir in Grand Marnier. Use to brush on cake layers.

Whipped-Cream Frosting

Makes enough to fill and frost a 9-inch, 4-layer cake

Mam Papaul bought a yellow Sunbeam mixer in the 1930s, and she used it until the day she died in 1967.

3 cups heavy whipping cream
½ cup powdered sugar

3 teaspoons unflavored gelatin
4 tablespoons water

1. Whip cream with powdered sugar at medium-high mixer speed until cream holds soft peaks.
2. Place gelatin in a small glass bowl and stir in water. Microwave 30 seconds. Slowly add gelatin mixture to whipped cream and continue whipping until cream holds stiff peaks. Frosting is now ready to spread on cake.

Blackberry Cobbler

Makes 8 servings

This was a rare summertime treat, since Mom liked to keep her berries to make jelly for jellyrolls and dumplings. She would surprise us with a dish of blackberries with sugar and cream only one morning during the summer, and that was it.

Blackberry Filling

1 quart blackberries
1½ cups sugar

1 cup water
3 tablespoons cornstarch

Batter

2 cups all-purpose flour
4 tablespoons sugar
3 teaspoons baking powder

½ teaspoon salt
4 tablespoons (½ stick) cold butter
1 cup milk

Whipped cream or vanilla ice cream for serving

1. Preheat oven to 375°F. Place blackberries, sugar, water, and cornstarch in a large saucepan set over medium heat. Stir and cook until filling thickens, about 4 minutes. Pour into a 9×13-inch casserole dish. Set aside.
2. To make batter, place flour, sugar, baking powder, and salt in a mixing bowl. Use a pastry blender to cut butter into dry mix until it resembles small peas. Stir in milk.
3. Scoop and drop batter onto hot filling. Bake until lightly browned, 25–30 minutes. Serve warm with whipped cream or ice cream.

Oatmeal Cake with Coconut Frosting

Makes 12 servings

Although I grew up on oatmeal and condensed milk for breakfast (and I still love it), this cake makes me fall in love with oatmeal over and over again. You will, too.

1¼ cups boiling water
1 cup quick-cooking oatmeal
½ cup (1 stick) butter or margarine,
    softened
1½ cups brown sugar

½ cup white sugar
2 large eggs
1 teaspoon vanilla extract
1½ cups all-purpose or cake flour
1 teaspoon baking soda

Coconut Frosting

1 cup grated or shredded coconut
½ cup (1 stick) butter, melted
½ cup brown sugar

4 tablespoons evaporated milk
1 teaspoon vanilla extract

1. Preheat oven to 350°F. Grease a 9×13-inch baking pan. Mix together boiling water, oatmeal, and butter in a large mixer bowl. Cover and let stand 20 minutes.
2. After 20 minutes, add brown sugar, white sugar, eggs, and vanilla. Beat well. Sift together remaining ingredients. Add to oatmeal mixture. Mix well.
3. Pour into prepared pan and bake until center springs back when lightly touched, about 30–35 minutes.
4. Remove cake from oven and lower oven temperature to 325°F. Make topping in a medium bowl by mixing together coconut frosting ingredients. Spread on top of warm oatmeal cake. Place cake back in oven and leave in until lightly browned, about 10 minutes. Serve warm or at room temperature, plain or with a dab of whipped cream.

Lelia's Doberge Cake

Makes 8 servings

This eight-layer cake inspired me to make a commercial line of multilayered velvet cakes and frosting mixes that I sold under the Mam Papaul brand name. Doberge cake has been a favorite birthday cake in New Orleans since the 1940s, when a pastry chef named Beulah Ledner created the original confection, which she based on the multilayered Hungarian dobos cake. Ledner's pastries were reflective of the German influence on New Orleans cooking, so that's why I'm including this cake. I don't know where my mom got this recipe, but she made it often, and we loved it.

½ cup (1 stick) butter
½ cup vegetable shortening
2 cups sugar
¼ teaspoon salt
4 large eggs, separated

3 cups sifted all-purpose flour
3 teaspoons baking powder
½ cup milk
½ cup water
1 teaspoon vanilla extract

Filling

4 squares unsweetened chocolate
1 quart whole milk
¾ cup all-purpose flour

1½ cups sugar
2 large eggs, lightly beaten

Chocolate Glaze

½ cup butter
4 squares unsweetened chocolate

2 cups sifted powdered sugar
½ cup boiling water

1. Preheat oven to 350°F. Line bottoms of 4 (8-inch) round cake pans with waxed paper. In a large bowl, cream together butter, shortening, sugar, and salt until light and fluffy, about 3 minutes. Add egg yolks and blend until smooth.
2. In a medium bowl, sift together flour and baking powder. In another bowl, mix together milk, water, and vanilla. Add flour mixture to butter mixture alternately with milk mixture, beginning and ending with flour.
3. Beat egg whites until stiff. Fold into cake batter. Pour even amounts of batter into prepared cake pans. Bake until firmly set, 20–25 minutes. Cool 2 minutes in pans. Remove from pans. Cool and split each layer horizontally.

4. To make filling, melt chocolate in a medium saucepan set over low heat. Add milk and bring to a boil over medium heat. Remove from heat.
5. Combine flour and sugar in a bowl and stir in a small amount of hot chocolate mixture. Whisk in beaten eggs. Add flour/egg mixture to hot liquid in saucepan. Return pan to heat and cook on medium until thick, about 5 minutes. Spread filling evenly between the 8 cake layers.
6. To make glaze, melt butter and chocolate in a small saucepan on low heat. Remove from heat and blend in sugar and water and beat until smooth. When glaze reaches spreading consistency, frost entire cake.

Shortcut Sour Cream Pound Cake
Makes 12 servings

Every era has several novelty cakes that are innovations on longtime favorites and become classic, such as this recipe.

1 (15.25-ounce) box yellow cake mix	¾ cup vegetable oil
4 large eggs	½ cup sugar
8 ounces sour cream	

Filling

¾ cup chopped pecans	3 teaspoons cinnamon
½ cup light brown sugar	

Glaze

1 cup powdered sugar	3 tablespoons whole milk
3 tablespoons butter	1 teaspoon vanilla extract

1. Preheat oven to 325°F. Butter and flour a Bundt pan well. In a large bowl, mix cake mix, eggs, sour cream, oil, and sugar on medium mixer speed 5 minutes. Pour half of batter into prepared Bundt pan.
2. Mix filling ingredients together and pour over batter in pan. Pour remaining cake batter on top of filling. Bake until cake springs back when lightly touched, about 1 hour.
3. Cool in pan 10 minutes before inverting onto a cooling rack. While cake is still warm, mix together glaze ingredients and pour over cake. Cool to room temperature.

Old-Fashioned Devil's Food Cake
with Pecan Divinity Frosting
Makes 8 servings

My mom frosted this Sunday dessert cake and then covered it with lots of chopped pecans—the more, the better. I found this recipe handwritten on the inner cover of my mom's old *Culinary Arts Institute Encyclopedic Cookbook*.

⅓ cup vegetable shortening (Mom used Crisco.)

1⅓ cups brown sugar

2 large eggs

2 cups sifted cake flour

⅔ cup cocoa

1½ teaspoons fresh baking powder (not more than 6 months old)

½ teaspoon salt

1 cup whole milk

1½ teaspoons vanilla extract

Pecan Divinity Frosting (*recipe follows*)

1. Preheat oven to 350°F. Grease and flour two (8-inch) round cake pans. Use medium mixer speed to cream together shortening and sugar until light and fluffy, about 3 minutes. Add eggs one at a time, beating well after each addition.
2. In a medium bowl, sift together flour, cocoa, baking powder, and salt. In a separate bowl, mix together milk and vanilla. Add dry ingredients to batter alternately with milk mixture, beginning and ending with dry ingredients.
3. Divide batter between the two prepared pans. Bake until cake springs back when lightly touched, about 30 minutes. Cool 5 minutes in pans before inverting onto a rack to cool completely.
4. Fill and frost cake layers with pecan divinity frosting, and feel free to press on extra gobs of pecans.

Pecan Divinity Frosting

Makes enough to fill and frost an 8-inch, 2-layer cake

3 cups sugar
¾ cup water
½ cup white corn syrup
¼ teaspoon salt

⅛ teaspoon cream of tartar
3 large egg whites
1 teaspoon vanilla extract
1 cup chopped pecans, divided*

1. Place first five ingredients in a heavy 1-quart saucepan and stir well. Bring to a boil over low heat without stirring. Cook to 240°F.
2. In a large bowl, beat egg whites until stiff. Slowly pour syrup over egg whites, beating constantly with mixer on medium-low speed.
3. Stir in vanilla. Add ¾ cup pecans and mix well. Frost cake. Sprinkle remaining ¼ cup pecans onto top of frosted cake.

*½ cup shredded coconut can be used in place of pecans.

Lelia with one of her mouth-watering sheet cakes

Carrot Cake with Cream Cheese Frosting

Makes 9 servings

Carrot cake became popular when I was in college in the 1960s. This cake is extremely moist and was the first I ever tasted with cream cheese frosting.

1½ cups sugar
¾ cup vegetable oil
3 large eggs, at room temperature
2 teaspoons vanilla extract
2 teaspoons vinegar
¾ cup milk
2 cups all-purpose flour
2 teaspoons baking soda

¼ teaspoon salt
¼ teaspoon freshly grated nutmeg (optional)
2½ cups grated carrots
1 cup crushed pineapple, well-drained
1 cup raisins (optional)
Cream Cheese Frosting (*recipe follows*)

1. Preheat oven to 350°F. Butter and flour a 9×13-inch baking pan or a 12-cup Bundt pan. Cream together sugar and oil on medium mixer speed for 3 minutes. Add eggs one at a time, beating well after each addition. Add vanilla and vinegar. Beat until light and fluffy, about 2 more minutes.
2. Sift together flour, baking soda, salt, and nutmeg. Add to creamed ingredients, beating at low mixer speed until blended. Stir in carrots, pineapple, and raisins.
3. Pour batter into prepared pan. Bake until cake springs back when lightly touched, about 1 hour. Cool completely and frost with Cream Cheese Frosting.

Cream Cheese Frosting

Makes enough to frost the top of a 9×13-inch cake

1½ (1-pound) boxes powdered sugar
1 (8-ounce) package cream cheese

½ cup (1 stick) butter
1 teaspoon vanilla extract

Beat together all ingredients until light and fluffy. Add a little milk if frosting is too stiff to spread. Frost cake immediately.

Mam Papaul's Chocolate Fudge Cake

Makes 12–16 servings

Whenever Mam Papaul heard a pregnant relative or child of a friend say she had an *envie* (pronounced on-vee), a craving, for a food, she was quick to satisfy that longing. It was never pickles and ice cream. Often it was chocolate cake or cream puffs. Her fear was that the child would be born with a birthmark if the *envie* was not satisfied.

This cake is great for a party and is always a hit. Fudge cake, along with traditional cookies, is always part of our family's Christmas.

1 cup (2 sticks) butter
⅓ cup Hershey's Special Dark Cocoa
2 cups sugar
1½ cups all-purpose flour

4 large eggs
1 cup chopped pecans
1½ teaspoons vanilla extract
Pinch salt

Topping

1 (10-ounce) package regular-sized
   marshmallows
½ cup (1 stick) butter
⅓ cup Hershey's Special Dark Cocoa
1 pound powdered sugar

⅓ cup milk
1 teaspoon vanilla extract
Pinch salt
½ cup chopped pecans

1. Preheat oven to 350°F. Grease a 9×13-inch baking pan. Melt butter and cocoa over low heat. In a large bowl, use a spoon to mix together sugar, flour, eggs, pecans, vanilla, and salt. Beat until flour is mixed in well.
2. Add cocoa and butter mixture to flour mixture. Beat well by hand. Pour into prepared pan and bake until center springs back when lightly touched, about 40 minutes. Remove from oven and leave in pan. Cover with topping while cake is still hot.
3. To make topping, cut marshmallows in half. Place marshmallows on top of hot cake. Melt butter with cocoa in a saucepan set over low heat, or in a microwave oven in a 2-quart bowl for about 1½ minutes. Remove from heat and stir in powdered sugar, milk, vanilla, and salt. Beat well and drizzle over marshmallows. Sprinkle with pecans. Let cake cool completely before serving.

Louisiana Gâteau de Sirop
(Louisiana Cane Syrup Cake)
Makes 12 servings

When I was in middle school, I remember one particular local wedding at which an older man quietly married a lady who was quite a bit younger. On the night of the wedding, the community had a *charivari* (pronounced cha-ree-va-ree), meaning that everyone drove their cars into the couple's yard and blew their horns and banged on pots and pans. *Charivari* is an old French custom, practiced in France since pagan times, that is supposed to drive evil spirits away from newlyweds.

With all the sugarcane fields in the region, there was never a shortage of sugar or cane syrup in any of the homes on the German Coast. My dad used to tell us that when he was a child, supper was sometimes just bread, milk, and syrup. This syrup cake would have been a good one to make to celebrate a *charivari*.

1 cup sugar
½ cup (1 stick) butter, slightly
   softened
3 large eggs
2 cups cane syrup
4 cups all-purpose flour

2 teaspoons baking soda
1 teaspoon cinnamon
¾ teaspoon freshly grated nutmeg
½ teaspoon ground cloves
1 cup whole milk

1. Preheat oven to 350°F. Butter and flour a 9×13-inch pan or a Bundt cake pan.
2. In a large bowl, cream together sugar and butter by hand. Add eggs one at a time and beat well after each addition. Beat in syrup.
3. Sift together flour, baking soda, cinnamon, nutmeg, and cloves. Add flour mixture to butter mixture alternately with milk, beating well after each addition. Pour and spread into prepared pan. Bake until cake springs back when lightly touched, about 1 hour. Cool cake completely before serving.

Chocolate Cobbler Cake

Makes 8 to 10 servings

I developed this cake for a demonstration requested by my chapter of the Delta Kappa Gamma Society. I wanted something easy and rich to go with our lunch, and this fit the bill. *Louisiana Kitchen and Culture* magazine published my recipe in 2015.

4 large eggs
1 cup chocolate morsels
1 cup chopped pecans
1 cup light or dark corn syrup
¾ cup light or dark brown sugar
1 tablespoon vanilla extract
1 teaspoon instant-coffee granules
  (optional)

½ teaspoon salt
¼ teaspoon freshly grated nutmeg
Whipped cream, ice cream, or
  cream cheese whipped with one
  tablespoon cream for serving

Topping

½ cup biscuit baking mix, or ½ cup
  self-rising flour blended with
  1 tablespoon butter
3 tablespoons sugar

½ cup whole or evaporated milk
½ cup toasted chopped pecans, plus
  additional for garnish

1. Preheat oven to 325°F. Grease a 9×13-inch casserole dish. Place all cake ingredients in a large bowl. Mix well by hand and pour into greased dish.
2. Prepare topping in a small bowl by mixing together biscuit mix and sugar. Mix in milk and pour over uncooked cake batter. Top with pecans. Bake until the top looks set, about 45 minutes. Serve cake warm with whipped cream, ice cream, or whipped cream cheese and chopped pecans.

Silver Wedding Cake

Makes 8–10 servings

This has been the favorite type of wedding cake on the German Coast for more years than I can remember. Almond flavor is synonymous with this cake, and the buttercream frosting is always made with real butter and pure almond and vanilla extracts (no imitations). In my day, wedding cakes were always homemade. My mom and Mam Papaul were famous for their wedding cakes, and they were honored when family and friends requested that they bake them. This recipe is adapted from an old Lever Brothers Company handout that was given to home economic teachers back in the 1960s. I was a home economics teacher back then.

2 cups sifted cake flour
1¼ cups sugar
3½ teaspoons baking powder
1 teaspoon salt
1 cup less 2 tablespoons milk
½ cup vegetable shortening

3 large egg whites, unbeaten
1 teaspoon pure almond extract
1 teaspoon pure vanilla extract
Almond Buttercream Frosting
   (recipe follows)

1. Preheat oven to 350°F. Line the bottoms of 2 (8-inch) round cake pans with parchment paper.
2. Sift together flour, sugar, baking powder, and salt into a large mixing bowl. Beat in half of milk and all of the shortening. Add half of remaining milk. Add egg whites, extracts, and remaining milk and beat on low mixer speed until light and fluffy, about 2 minutes.
3. Place equal amounts of batter into prepared pans. Bake until center springs back when touched lightly, 25–30 minutes. Remove from pans after 5 minutes and cool completely. Fill and frost with Almond Buttercream Frosting.

Almond Buttercream Frosting

Makes enough to frost and fill one 8-inch layer cake

1 pound powdered sugar
½ cup (1 stick) butter
4 tablespoons vegetable shortening

3 tablespoons water
½ teaspoon almond extract
½ teaspoon vanilla extract

Place all ingredients in a large mixing bowl. Blend together at low mixer speed and beat on medium until light and fluffy, about 3 minutes. Spread immediately on cake.

When I was growing up, the backyard was the site of all manner of activity, including wedding receptions, the boucherie, seafood boils, and always the children's playground. This photo captures Bert and Diana Songy's wedding, April 17, 1948. I am the flower girl second from the left.

Classic Cheesecake

Makes 8 servings

This is a basic cheesecake that can be flavored to your liking or topped with fruit or sour cream. When my three daughters were in 4-H clubs, they made several variations to enter in the organization's egg cookery contest. Sometimes they even won.

Crust

30 chocolate cream sandwich cookies, blended into crumbs

¼ cup (4 tablespoons) butter, melted

Cake

5 (8-ounce) packages cream cheese
2 cups sugar
6 large eggs
1 cup sour cream

½ cup all-purpose flour
1 tablespoon of your favorite flavored extract (vanilla, almond, lemon, etc.)

1. Preheat oven to 325°F. Make crust by mixing cookie crumbs and butter together and pressing into the bottom of a 9-inch springform pan.
2. In a large bowl, blend cream cheese with sugar on low mixer speed just until smooth. (Overbeating will incorporate too much air and will cause the cake to crack.)
3. Add eggs one at a time, beating well after each addition. Do not overbeat. (Again, too much air in the batter will cause the cake to crack.) Add remaining ingredients and mix well on low speed.
4. Pour filling into crust. Place pan on a 12×12-inch piece of aluminum foil. Press foil up the sides of the pan. Place pan in a 2-inch warm-water bath (a larger baking pan with warm water that reaches 1 inch up the sides). Bake until cake is just set, 1–1¼ hours. Turn oven off and cool cake completely in closed oven. Remove rim and refrigerate 1 hour or until cold.

Divinity Angel Roll

Makes 10 servings

This cake is based on divinity fudge, a favorite candy on the German Coast. I developed this recipe when I was in high school, and it has become a staple at birthday parties. Although I do bake from scratch most of the time, for this cake I start with an angel food cake mix. My daughter-in-law recently reminded me that she *really* likes the divinity angel roll I used to make for her birthday. So, in the future, I will not be remiss in making this special cake for her birthday.

1 (16-ounce) box angel food cake mix, plus ingredients called for on box

Frosting

3 egg whites

2 cups sugar

½ cup water

2 tablespoons white corn syrup

Pinch cream of tartar

2 teaspoons pure almond extract

¼ cup chopped, toasted almonds

   (optional)

1. Preheat oven to 375°F. Line the bottom of a jellyroll pan with wax or parchment paper. Mix cake according to directions on box and pour into prepared pan. Bake until lightly browned, or until the top springs back when lightly touched, about 18 minutes.
2. To make frosting, beat egg whites until stiff. Set aside. Place sugar, water, corn syrup, and cream of tartar in a heavy, 2-quart pot. Mix well and boil over medium heat to soft ball stage, 235–240°F.
3. Using a mixer on medium speed, beat ½ of the syrup mixture into the egg whites. Continue cooking remainder of the syrup mixture to hard crack stage, 300–310°F (when a few drops of syrup are dropped into a cup of water, the sugar will be hard and brittle). Beat this syrup and almond extract into egg whites for 5 minutes.
4. Spread ¾ of frosting evenly over angel food cake slab. From the long side, roll cake jellyroll fashion. Spread top of cake with remaining frosting and garnish with almonds. Slice and serve.

Vanilla Wafer Cake

Makes 10 servings

This is one of the things we did with vanilla wafers other than make banana pudding. It's a very dense cake, and it is so rich and so good I just couldn't leave it out of this cookbook.

2 cups sugar

1 cup (2 sticks) butter or margarine

6 large eggs

1 (12-ounce) box vanilla wafers, crushed in a food processor or with a rolling pin

½ cup whole milk

1 cup chopped pecans

1 (7-ounce) package flaked coconut

1 teaspoon vanilla extract

Whipped cream or ice cream for serving

1. Preheat oven to 350°F. Butter and flour a tube or Bundt pan. Using medium mixer speed, cream together sugar and butter until light and fluffy, about 3 minutes. Beat eggs in one at a time. Beat mixture well, about 2 more minutes.
2. Stir crushed vanilla wafers into butter mixture, alternating with the milk. Add pecans, coconut, and vanilla. Beat well.
3. Bake in prepared pan until center is completely set, 1½ hours. Serve warm with whipped cream or ice cream.

Gingerbread Cake

Makes 12 servings

This spicy cake was an after-school treat we all enjoyed. It was one of my dad's favorite desserts; I think it reminded him of his childhood. Nothing is better than a piece of warm gingerbread with a glass of ice-cold boiled milk. Yes, we boiled the milk from Sally, our backyard cow. Boiling took the place of pasteurization in those days. When raw milk is boiled, a layer of cream settles on the top. Delicious.

1½ teaspoons baking soda
1½ teaspoons cinnamon
1½ teaspoons ginger
¾ teaspoon salt
½ teaspoon powdered cloves
½ cup butter, softened
½ cup sugar

1 large egg
1 cup molasses
2½ cups sifted all-purpose flour
1 cup hot water
½ cup raisins (optional)
3 tablespoons powdered sugar

1. Preheat oven to 350°F. Butter and flour a 9×13-inch baking pan. In a medium bowl, sift together baking soda, cinnamon, ginger, salt, and cloves. In a large bowl, use medium mixer speed to beat together butter, sugar, and egg until light and fluffy, about 3 minutes. Add molasses and beat well.
2. Beat in flour and hot water alternately. Stir in raisins.
3. Pour batter into prepared pan. Bake until cake springs back when lightly touched, about 1 hour. Cool 5 minutes and remove from pan. Cool completely on a rack.
4. Fancy up this plain cake by placing a rectangular doily on the cooled cake and sift powdered sugar over the doily to make a lacy sugar topping.

Breakfast Sausage Spice Cake

Makes 8–10 servings

This sounds like a creation from a boucherie, but it is not. A good friend and neighbor made this cake for me before we moved back to Louisiana from California, where my husband worked as an FBI agent. Over the years, I've made a few changes to her recipe, and this cake always makes an interesting addition to a breakfast menu. I serve it buttered with cups of hot coffee.

2 cups boiling water
1 cup raisins
1 pound bulk pork sausage
1½ cups dark-brown sugar
1½ cups white sugar
2 large eggs, slightly beaten
3 cups all-purpose flour, sifted
1 teaspoon ground ginger

1 teaspoon baking powder
¼ teaspoon allspice
¼ teaspoon freshly grated nutmeg
¼ teaspoon ground mace
1 teaspoon baking soda
1 cup strong cold coffee
1 cup chopped pecans

1. Preheat oven to 350°F. Grease and flour a Bundt pan well. Add boiling water and raisins to a small bowl. Let stand 5 minutes. Drain raisins well and dry on paper towels or a clean cloth.
2. Meanwhile, in a large mixing bowl, combine sausage, brown sugar, and white sugar. Stir until mixture is well blended. Add eggs and beat well.
3. On waxed paper or a paper plate, sift together flour, ginger, baking powder, allspice, nutmeg, and mace. In a small bowl, stir baking soda into coffee.
4. Add flour mixture and coffee mixture alternately into meat mixture, beating well after each addition. Add soaked raisins and pecans to batter. Pour into prepared pan. Bake until top is light brown and springs back when touched, about 1½ hours. Cool 15 minutes before removing from pan. Serve slightly warm.

Bread Pudding with Meringue

Makes 6 servings

We always topped our bread pudding with meringue, and we never served it with a sauce. Although stale French bread is best for a bread pudding, any leftover stale bread or doughnuts will work. As an adult, I like to top my breading with a little Grand Marnier.

5 cups cubed, stale French bread
3 cups whole milk
1½ cups light-brown or white sugar
4 tablespoons (½ stick) butter, melted
¼ cup or more raisins, or 1 cup
    canned fruit cocktail, drained

3 large egg yolks, slightly beaten
½ teaspoon cinnamon, or 1 teaspoon
    vanilla extract
¼ teaspoon salt

Meringue

3 large egg whites
Pinch cream of tartar
5 tablespoons granulated sugar

½ teaspoon almond extract
½ teaspoon vanilla extract

1. Preheat oven to 350°F. In a large bowl, add all pudding ingredients. Stir well, making sure bread cubes are soaked well with liquid. Pour into an 8×8-inch casserole dish and bake until slightly puffy and brown, 45–55 minutes. Remove from oven and turn temperature up to 400°F.
2. As soon as the bread pudding comes out of the oven, make meringue by first washing beaters and a medium bowl with dish detergent and hot water. Rinse with hot water. Beat egg whites and cream of tartar until frothy. Add sugar, one tablespoon at a time. Beat until stiff. Add almond and vanilla extracts.
3. Spread meringue on top of hot bread pudding, making sure edges are sealed to the dish. Place in hot oven until brown, about 2–3 minutes. Serve warm.

Tarte à la Bouille
(Boiled Vanilla Custard Pie)
Makes 6 servings

For Pépère Zoot's birthday, which was March 19, St. Joseph's Day, Mam Papaul always made *tarte à la bouille*, a boiled custard pie baked in a sweet dough crust. I don't remember her making it at any other time. I like to use a clear, oven-safe pie dish so I can check the browning of the bottom crust. Pépère Zoot was married to my mémère, Clarice Keller, and he lived through the assassinations of Presidents Lincoln, Garfield, McKinley, and Kennedy. I remember him sitting on a swing in his front yard visiting with friends, with muscadine grapevines trailing overhead. Fat, juicy muscadines are indigenous to Louisiana.

Sweet Pastry for Crust

1 cup, plus 2 tablespoons sugar	½ teaspoon vanilla extract
5 tablespoons butter or margarine	1¾ cups all-purpose flour
1 large egg	1 teaspoon baking powder
2 tablespoons milk	¾ teaspoon salt

Filling

2 cups whole milk	2 large egg yolks
½ cup sugar	1 tablespoon butter
2 tablespoons cornstarch	1 teaspoon vanilla extract
Pinch salt	

1. To make crust, in a large bowl using medium mixer speed beat together sugar, butter, and egg until light and fluffy, about 2 minutes. Blend in milk and vanilla.
2. In a separate medium bowl, sift together flour, baking powder, and salt. Blend into the creamed mixture. Divide dough in two, roll into balls, and wrap in foil. Refrigerate 2 hours.
3. Roll out one dough ball to fit an 8-inch pie pan with a ½-inch overlap. Roll out second ball of dough to a 12-inch circle. Cut into strips and weave into a lattice to fit the top of the pie. Place both pieces of pie dough between damp cloths and refrigerate until ready to use.

4. To make filling, place milk, sugar, cornstarch, and salt in a heavy-bottomed, 2-quart pot. Cook on low heat, stirring constantly, until mixture comes to a boil. Cook an additional 2 minutes, stirring occasionally.
5. Beat egg yolks in a small bowl. Add several tablespoons of hot custard to egg yolks, stirring constantly. Add butter and vanilla. Stir well and add to custard in pot. Cook over low heat until thick, about 3 minutes. Spread in a shallow, buttered dish to cool.
6. Preheat oven to 375°F. Pour cooled filling into pie shell. Place lattice on top of pie and trim and crimp. Bake until crust is light golden brown.

Easy Cherry Pie with Almond Glaze

Makes 1 (9-inch) pie

I first made this pie for a 4-H contest when I was in the ninth grade. I taught a friend to make it, and she beat me in the contest. Humph. This is a shortcut version of the original recipe.

2 refrigerated pie crusts
1 (21-ounce) can cherry pie filling
¾ cup powdered sugar

1 tablespoon water
½ teaspoon almond extract

1. Preheat oven to 400°F. Fit 1 pie crust into the bottom of a 9-inch pie pan. Bake 10 minutes.
2. Place pie filling into precooked crust. Roll second crust into a 12-inch circle and cut into ½-inch strips. Construct a lattice and place on top of pie. Trim to fit and crimp edges. Bake until lightly browned, about 35 minutes.
3. In a small bowl, mix together powdered sugar, water, and almond extract. Drizzle over warm pie, slice, and serve.

Mémère's Li'l Coconut Pies

Makes 10 hand pies

When I returned home from school, if I found my mémère sitting on the front porch grating a fresh coconut, I knew what she was up to—little coconut pies. These folded hand pies are a labor of love. Have you ever tried to crack a coconut and remove the meat? Not an easy job. After that, the coconut meat has to be grated by hand. You can still find these little pies in mom-and-pop restaurants and convenience stores on River Road. On a recent All Saints' Day I bought some, along with chicken and andouille gumbo (which tasted like the Mam Papaul mix), in a cemetery at a fund-raiser in Edgard. Everyone along the river calls these sweet treats "li'l coconut pies."

Filling

2½ cups freshly grated coconut (You can cheat and use 2 [17-ounce] cans of drained Ancel-brand coconut in syrup; do not add sugar and water.)

2 cups sugar
1½ cups water

Egg wash for pastry

1 large egg

2 tablespoons water

Pastry

3 cups sifted all-purpose flour
1 teaspoon salt
1¼ cups shortening, lard, or butter

5 tablespoons ice-cold water
1 tablespoon vinegar

1. Place all filling ingredients in a heavy, 3-quart pot. Stir and bring to a boil over medium-high heat and cook until sugar is dissolved. Lower heat and simmer 16 to 18 minutes or until coconut is clear and syrup has thickened. Drain coconut and place in a buttered, heat-safe dish to cool. (Drained syrup may be used on biscuits, pancakes, or waffles.)
2. Combine egg wash ingredients in a small bowl and set aside.
3. To make pastry, preheat oven to 375°F. In a large bowl, whisk together flour and salt. Use a pastry blender to cut in shortening. Make a well in the center of the flour mixture. Add ice water and vinegar and gently mix with

a large spoon. Place dough on a clean, well-floured dishcloth. Use dishcloth to form a ball with dough. Use dough immediately, or wrap in foil or plastic wrap and refrigerate until ready to use.

4. Divide dough into 10 pieces and roll out each piece into a 5-inch circle, about ⅛ inch thick. Brush edges lightly with water.

5. Place a tablespoon of coconut filling in center of each circle of dough. Fold one side over onto the other and crimp edges with a fork to seal.

6. Brush top of each pie with egg wash. Place pies on a baking sheet and bake until lightly browned, about 10 minutes. Serve at room temperature.

Mémère

Pumpkin Pie

Makes 1 (9-inch) pie or 12 mini pies

Condensed milk adds another layer of flavor to this sweet and spicy pumpkin pie. Of course, we loved anything sweetened with condensed milk. I made this pie recently at the request of my precious five-year-old grandson, Riley. I was happy to see him eat it with great gusto; as he bit into the pie, he flashed me a grin.

2 cups cooked fresh or canned pumpkin
1 (14-ounce) can sweetened condensed milk (not evaporated milk)
2 large eggs

2 teaspoons pumpkin pie spice, or 1 teaspoon cinnamon, ½ teaspoon freshly grated nutmeg, ½ teaspoon ginger, ¼ teaspoon cloves, and ¼ teaspoon mace
1 teaspoon vanilla extract
¼ teaspoon salt
1 unbaked 9-inch pastry shell

1. Preheat oven to 400°F. Combine all filling ingredients in a large bowl. Blend well to combine, being sure eggs are well incorporated.
2. Bake pastry shell 15 minutes. Remove from oven and pour in filling.
3. Reduce heat to 350°F. Place pie in oven and bake until a knife comes out clean when inserted into pie, about 35 minutes. Cool completely at room temperature and refrigerate.

Pecan Pie

Makes 1 (9-inch) pie

As a child, I loved picking pecans from the tree in our backyard. Sometimes we had so many that I could sit on the ground and pick up the ones that lay around me. Our pecan tree had a rope swing that we all loved. Everyone I know has a favorite recipe for pecan pie, and this simple one is mine.

1 cup sugar
½ cup (1 stick) butter
1 cup dark corn syrup
4 large eggs

1 teaspoon vanilla extract
1 cup pecans, halves or pieces
1 unbaked 9-inch pie crust, homemade or ready-made

1. Preheat oven to 350°F. In a large bowl, use medium mixer speed to beat together sugar and butter until well combined. Stir in corn syrup, eggs, and vanilla. Add pecans.
2. Pour filling into pie shell and bake until filling is set, about 50 minutes. Cool completely at room temperature.

Grasshopper Pie
Makes 1 (9-inch) pie

I love all things mint, and this is one of my favorite mint desserts. I learned to make this pie when I lived in California. My husband and I enjoyed it at an anniversary dinner at Tail of the Cock, a restaurant in Westwood. This recipe is too good to leave out.

Crust

24 chocolate-cream sandwich cookies, finely crushed

¼ cup (½ stick) butter or margarine, melted

Filling

1 pint jar marshmallow cream, or 24 regular-sized marshmallows
½ cup whole milk

¼ cup crème de menthe liqueur
2 tablespoons white crème de cocoa
1 cup whipping cream

1. Combine cookie crumbs and butter and press into the bottom of a 9-inch springform pan, reserving 3 tablespoons to use as a garnish.
2. In a small saucepan set over medium-low heat, melt marshmallow cream with milk. Blend in crème de menthe and crème de cocoa. Set aside to cool.
3. Beat whipping cream until stiff. Add to cooled marshmallow mixture. Pour into pie crust. Garnish top of pie with reserved chocolate crumbs. Freeze until firm enough to cut, at least 2 hours. Remove from freezer 15 minutes before serving.

Mam Papaul's Li'l Dry Tea Cakes

Makes 60 cookies

Tea cakes aren't really cakes; they're cookies. Mam Papaul's tea cakes are thin and dry, good for dipping in milk or coffee. More traditional tea cakes (as in the following recipe) are thick and cakey.

1 cup (2 sticks) butter or vegetable
   shortening
1 cup sugar
2 large eggs, beaten
2 drops anise oil, or 2 teaspoons
   crushed anise seeds
1 teaspoon vanilla extract

5 cups cake flour
2 teaspoons baking powder
1¼ teaspoons salt
1 teaspoon baking soda
1 cup sour cream
Lemon Glaze (*recipe follows*)

1. In a large bowl, use medium mixer speed to cream together butter, sugar, eggs, anise oil, and vanilla.
2. Sift together flour, baking powder, salt, and baking soda. Add flour mixture to butter mixture alternately with sour cream. Chill at least 1 hour.
3. Preheat oven to 350°F. Roll dough out to ¼-inch thickness and cut with cookie cutters. Place on a greased cookie sheet. Bake until lightly browned, about 15 minutes. Cool on a rack and frost with lemon glaze or your favorite powdered-sugar frosting.

Lemon Glaze

Makes ⅔ cup

1½ cups powdered sugar
1 tablespoon or more freshly
   squeezed lemon juice

1–2 tablespoons water

Combine ingredients to make a thin glaze. Great on cookies and pound cakes.

Traditional Tea Cakes

Makes 3–4 dozen

If any cookie is generic to the area, it is the tea cake. Each family has its own recipe that has been handed down for generations. These are delicious plain, but for a bit of sweet goodness, glaze them with a light frosting. My friend Dolores Chauffe generously shared this recipe.

½ cup (1 stick) butter
1 cup sugar
2 large eggs
2 tablespoons vanilla extract or
    lemon juice

4 cups sifted all-purpose flour
4 teaspoons baking powder
6 tablespoons milk

Glaze

2 cups powdered sugar
2 tablespoons water (about)

2 teaspoons lemon juice
½ teaspoon vanilla or almond extract

1. Preheat oven to 350°F. In a large bowl, cream together butter and sugar using medium mixer speed. Add eggs and vanilla and mix well.
2. Sift together flour and baking powder. Add flour mixture to butter mixture alternately with milk.
3. Roll onto a floured board to ¼-inch thickness. Cut out with any shape 3-inch cutter. Bake on an ungreased baking sheet until lightly browned, approximately 20 minutes. Remove to a rack and cool.
4. Combine glaze ingredients in a small bowl. Dip tops of tea cakes into glaze and place on a rack to dry.

Adeline's Icebox Cookies

Makes 30 cookies

When I was young, I called my aunt "Enty" because I couldn't say Aunt Adeline. Aunt Adeline was like a second mom to me. She and I shared recipes, as well as an interest in sewing. This was one of her favorite cookies; it is so easy and delicious.

1 cup (2 sticks) margarine or butter
2 cups light-brown sugar
2 large eggs

3¼ cups all-purpose flour
2 teaspoons vanilla extract
2 cups chopped pecans

1. In a large bowl, cream together margarine and sugar. Beat in eggs. Add flour and vanilla and beat well. Mix in pecans.
2. Divide dough into 2 pieces and shape each portion into a 2-inch-wide log. Wrap in foil and freeze until ready to bake.
3. Preheat oven to 350°F. Remove dough from freezer. Cut frozen dough into ½-inch slices. Bake on a lightly greased cookie sheet until edges are brown, about 10 minutes. Remove to a rack and cool.

Gingerbread Cookies

Makes 30 (3½-inch) gingerbread men

This molasses cookie tastes like what was known on the German Coast as a stage plank cookie. I made these for my dad and a couple of uncles who recalled enjoying stage planks in their childhood. My uncle Clancy in Florida also enjoyed making this recipe, and at least once a year he telephoned me for it. I don't know if he actually lost his copy of the recipe or just wanted to talk to someone from home. Doesn't matter—I always enjoyed his phone calls.

5¼ cups all-purpose flour, measure
    first and sift
1½ teaspoons cream of tartar
1½ teaspoons ginger
1½ teaspoon cinnamon
¾ teaspoon salt
½ teaspoon cloves

1 cup (2 sticks) butter or lard
1 cup sugar
1 large egg, beaten
2 teaspoons vanilla extract
4 teaspoons baking soda
¼ cup hot water
1 cup dark molasses or cane syrup

1. In a large bowl, sift together flour, cream of tartar, ginger, cinnamon, salt, and cloves.
2. In another large bowl, use medium mixer speed to cream together butter, sugar, egg, and vanilla.
3. Dissolve baking soda in hot water. Stir in molasses. Add to butter mixture and mix well. Stir in flour mixture until well blended. Cover with plastic wrap and chill in the refrigerator 20 minutes.
4. Preheat oven to 400°. Lightly grease a baking sheet and dust with flour. Roll out chilled dough on a hard, floured surface to ¼-inch thickness. Cut out with a cookie cutter and place on prepared baking sheet. Bake until edges start to turn brown, about 10 minutes. Cool on a wire rack.

Madeleines
Makes 18–24 cookies

This elegant soft cookie is a perfect complement to a cup of tea. And they're so good, it's hard to eat just one. With all the Meyer lemons that grow so easily in this part of Louisiana, I am surprised we do not have more lemon desserts.

2 large eggs
¼ cup (½ stick) butter, melted
3 tablespoons sugar
1 teaspoon lemon zest
¼ teaspoon freshly squeezed lemon juice

¼ teaspoon vanilla extract
3½ tablespoons cake flour
⅛ teaspoon baking powder
½ cup powdered sugar

1. Preheat oven to 350°F. Butter and flour madeleine pans. Using medium mixer speed, beat together eggs, butter, and sugar for 1 minute. Beat in lemon zest, lemon juice, and vanilla until just combined.
2. In a small bowl, sift together flour and baking powder. Gently blend flour mixture into the batter.
3. Fill each mold ½ full with batter. Bake until lightly browned, 10–12 minutes. Carefully remove from pan and let cool on a wire rack. Dust lightly with powdered sugar.

Crispy Oatmeal Raisin Cookies

Makes 4 dozen cookies

This is my son Tregg's favorite cookie. I made these for him and his college friends many times. I developed this recipe to add nutritional value to a cookie my children enjoyed.

½ cup (1 stick) butter
½ cup light-brown sugar
½ cup white granulated sugar
1 large egg
1 tablespoon water
½ teaspoon vanilla extract
1 cup rolled oats
1 cup all-purpose flour

½ teaspoon baking soda
¼ teaspoon salt
¼ teaspoon freshly grated nutmeg
¼ teaspoon cinnamon
¼ teaspoon allspice
2½ cups Kellogg's brand Rice
   Krispies cereal
⅓ cup raisins

1. Preheat oven to 350°F and grease a cookie sheet. In a large mixing bowl, use medium mixer speed to cream together butter, sugars, egg, water, and vanilla.
2. In a separate mixing bowl, mix together oats, flour, baking soda, salt, nutmeg, cinnamon, and allspice. Blend the oat mixture into the creamed mixture. When well blended, stir in Rice Krispies and raisins.
3. Using a 1-inch scoop or a teaspoon, drop balls of batter onto the prepared cookie sheet. Bake until lightly browned, 12–15 minutes. For a chewy cookie, bake less. For a crisper cookie, bake longer. Remove cookies to a wire rack and cool completely. Store in an airtight container.

Pecan Crunch Cookies

Makes 5 dozen

I made these cookies often for my brother when he went to Louisiana State University in Baton Rouge. Pecans are difficult to get out of their shells, so sometimes I shelled just enough to make one batch for him to take back to school.

1 cup white sugar
1 cup light-brown sugar
½ cup (1 stick) butter or shortening
2 large eggs
1 teaspoon vanilla extract

3 cups all-purpose flour
1 teaspoon baking soda
½ teaspoon salt
1 cup chopped pecans

1. In a large bowl, use medium mixer speed to cream together sugars, butter, eggs, and vanilla.
2. In another bowl, sift together flour, baking soda, and salt. Stir into sugar mixture and mix well. Cover with plastic wrap and chill 2 hours.
3. Preheat oven to 375°F. Grease cookie sheet. Mix pecans into chilled dough. Shape into ¾-inch balls and place 2 inches apart on a baking sheet. Flatten dough balls with bottom of a greased glass dipped in sugar. Bake until edges start to turn brown, 8–10 minutes. Remove to a wire rack and cool. Store in an airtight container.

Mam Papaul's Rocks

Makes 175 cookies

I often wonder where my mother and grandmother got the recipes for their large repertoire of sweets. They did not have home or public libraries full of recipe books like many of us enjoy today. Chances are good that many of the desserts my family made came from Mémère's early experience with her mother in the kitchen.

2 cups sugar
1 cup (2 sticks) butter or margarine
3 large eggs
2 tablespoons warm water
3½ cups all-purpose flour
1 teaspoon cinnamon

1 teaspoon freshly grated nutmeg
¼ teaspoon ginger
¼ teaspoon cloves
1 teaspoon baking soda
7 cups chopped pecans
2 pounds dates, chopped

1. Preheat oven to 350°F and grease a cookie sheet. In a large bowl, use medium mixer speed to cream together sugar and butter. Add eggs and water. Beat well.
2. In another bowl, sift together flour, spices, and baking soda. Stir into butter mixture. Stir in pecans and dates.
3. Using a 1-inch scoop or a teaspoon, drop batter onto prepared cookie sheet. Bake cookies until they start to turn brown, approximately 12 minutes. Cool on a wire rack and store in an airtight container.

Wine Cookies

Makes 2 dozen

These cookies are attractively shaped into scored crescents, and they're delicious with hot coffee or dipped in wine. This is my husband's favorite Italian cookie.

½ cup (1 stick) butter, softened
1⅓ cups light-brown sugar
1 large egg
2 tablespoons red wine
⅛ teaspoon almond extract

½ cup finely chopped blanched
  almonds
3 cups sifted all-purpose flour
¾ teaspoon cinnamon
½ teaspoon baking soda

1. Preheat oven to 400°F. In a large bowl, use medium mixer speed to cream together butter and sugar until light and fluffy. Beat in egg, wine, and almond extract.
2. Stir in almonds. Sift together flour, cinnamon, and baking soda. Add to egg mixture and mix well. Chill 2 hours.
3. Roll dough into ½-inch-thick, pencil-like logs. Cut each log into 2-inch pieces. Make 3 cuts ½ inch apart about halfway into each piece. Bend each to make a crescent. Place an inch apart on a cookie sheet.
4. Bake until edges start to turn brown, 10–12 minutes. Remove to a wire rack and let cool.

Sesame Seed Cookies

Makes 36–48 cookies

Although my friend Mrs. Jack Pizzolato gave me this recipe, it was my 100-year-old friend Mrs. Lena Bushalacci La Croix who gave me the secret to getting the seeds to stick to the cookie dough, and that's to roll the unbaked cookie in evaporated milk. I have since found out that other Italian friends use a sugar-water mixture.

2 pounds all-purpose flour
2 cups sugar
1 teaspoon baking powder
1 pound (4 sticks) butter
⅓ cup whole milk
2 large eggs

1 teaspoon vanilla extract
½ pound sesame seeds
1 (12-ounce) can evaporated milk,
   or 2 tablespoons sugar dissolved
   in 2 cups water

1. Preheat oven to 350°F. In a large bowl, sift together flour, sugar, and baking powder. Using a pastry blender or your fingers, work the butter into the flour mixture until it resembles small peas.
2. In a small bowl, beat together milk, eggs, and vanilla. Add to the flour mixture. Mix well and knead lightly. Roll dough to a ½-inch-thick rectangle and cut into ½-inch strips. Roll each strip to form a pencil-sized log.
3. Cut dough logs into 2-inch pieces. Dip each piece in evaporated milk, then roll in sesame seeds.
4. Bake cookies on a large ungreased cookie sheet until seeds are lightly toasted, about 20 minutes. Remove to a wire rack to cool.

Anise Caps

Makes 3–4 dozen

These little anise cookies are the ones I especially like on a St. Joseph's altar—an old Sicilian tradition of baking elaborate food offerings in thanksgiving to a favorite saint. Anise cookies go by many names, but most often they're called anise caps because, if done properly, they do look like little caps. Even though we associate this cookie with the Italians, Germans have something similar, called Anise Plaetzchen. I personally think this cookie is most likely of German origin, since it looks somewhat like the German Springerle. When I was a child and we went shopping on Canal Street in New Orleans, my mom often bought these for me from McKenzie's Bakery or the D. H. Holmes Department Store candy counter.

2 cups sugar
4 large eggs
4 drops anise oil, or 1½ teaspoons
  anise extract, or 2 teaspoons
  crushed anise seeds

¼ teaspoon baking powder
3 cups sifted cake flour
Multicolored sugar sprinkles

1. Preheat oven to 350°F. Grease a cookie sheet or line with parchment paper. In a large metal bowl, use medium mixer speed to beat together sugar and eggs for 10 minutes.
2. Make a double boiler by placing water in a pot, then placing the bowl of sugar and eggs on top of the pot. Bottom of bowl should not touch the water. Bring water to a boil and beat egg mixture with a whisk or portable hand mixer until it reaches 120°F. Add anise and mix well.
3. Remove bowl from pot and beat mixture 10 minutes. Stir baking powder into sifted cake flour. Gently fold flour/baking powder mixture into egg mixture.
4. Place batter in a pastry bag that has been fitted with a ½-inch plain or fancy tip. Drop quarter-size or smaller mounds of batter onto prepared cookie sheet. Top with multicolored sugar sprinkles. Set out overnight at room temperature.
5. The next day, heat oven to 350°F. Bake cookies until they form a cap, about 10 minutes. (Cookies should not be brown.) Remove to a wire rack and let cool.

Italian Fig Cookies

Makes enough cookies to feed an army

This is the one cookie that every Italian will tell you is a must-have on a St. Joseph's altar. Recipes abound, and each is a little different. This recipe is good for small fig cookies as well as large cakes (*cuccidati*) in shapes of religious significance.

Filling

3 pounds dried figs

2 pounds raisins

Juice and rinds of 2 medium oranges

⅓ cup whiskey

1 pound shelled pecans, chopped

2 teaspoons freshly grated nutmeg

2 teaspoons allspice

2 teaspoons ground black pepper

1. Place figs and raisins in a large bowl. Add orange juice and whiskey. Coarsely chop orange rinds and add to fig mixture. Stir in pecans, nutmeg, allspice, and black pepper. Cover and let stand at room temperature overnight.
2. The next day, chop everything in a food processor. Set aside and make dough.

Dough

5 pounds all-purpose flour

4 tablespoons baking powder

1 tablespoon salt

1½ pounds (6 sticks) butter or vegetable shortening

1 pound sugar

2½ cups warm water

4 eggs, lightly beaten

Colored sugar sprinkles

1. Preheat oven to 350°. In a very large bowl, sift together flour, baking powder, and salt. Use a pastry blender to work butter into the flour mixture until it looks like small peas.
2. Dissolve sugar in warm water. Cool and blend in beaten eggs.
3. Mix dry ingredients with wet ingredients. Knead until smooth. Divide dough into fourths. Roll each portion into a 15×12-inch rectangle that is ⅛ inch thick. Cut into 4-inch-long strips that are 3 inches wide.
4. Lay ½-inch logs of filling down the center of the strips. Moisten edges of dough and pinch sides to close. Cut into 1½-inch pieces. Bake until edges start to turn brown, about 10 minutes. Make glaze while cookies are cooling. Dip top of each in glaze and decorate with colored sprinkles.

Glaze

2 pounds powdered sugar
1 teaspoon vanilla extract

A few drops food coloring (any
bright color)
Water for thinning

Combine powdered sugar, vanilla, and food coloring with enough water to make a thin glaze.

Date Roll

Makes 12–18 slices

I remember this goodie from my childhood. It was particularly popular up the river near St. James Parish. Aunt Aurelie, my sister Joel's *nanan*, godmother, who lived in Vacherie, always made this for Christmas, and my sister was the one who had the foresight to get her recipe before she died.

2½ cups sugar
⅔ cup evaporated milk
1 pound dates, diced
4 cups chopped pecans

1 tablespoon butter
1 teaspoon vanilla extract
¼ teaspoon baking soda
Powdered sugar

1. Place sugar and milk in a heavy, 3-quart pot. Cook on medium heat to soft ball stage (270°F). Add dates and cook, stirring constantly, until mixture is a smooth mass.
2. Remove from heat and add pecans, butter, vanilla, and baking soda. Set aside until mixture is cool enough to handle.
3. Dust top of a table with a generous amount of powdered sugar. Roll date mixture in sugar to make a 2½-inch-wide log. Wrap in a damp cloth and place in refrigerator at least 2 hours. Remove cloth and cut into bite-sized pieces. Wrap pieces in waxed paper before storing in an airtight container.

Cream Puffs
Makes 12 large cream puffs

My daughter is a pastry chef, and she calls these by the French name, *profiteroles*. We called them cream puffs, and they were always filled with vanilla cream and sprinkled with powdered sugar. I have been making cream puffs since high school, where everyone thought of me as a good cook. The truth is that when I went off to college to study home economics, I could bake but not cook. When I graduated from college, I knew a lot about the chemistry of food but still could not cook. One time I wanted to surprise my parents with supper after they arrived home from a day in New Orleans. I tried to cook a frozen chuck roast in the broiler, which was a disaster. But my cream puffs were good.

This recipe is a classic, and I always double it. The *pâte à choux* can be used for éclairs as well as cream puffs.

Pâte à Choux

1½ cups water
¾ cups (1½ sticks) butter
1½ cups bread flour or all-purpose flour
6 large eggs

Vanilla Cream Filling (*recipe follows*), or whipped cream, or ice cream, for filling pastry shells
Powdered sugar for dusting

1. Preheat oven to 375°F and line a cookie sheet with parchment paper. Place water and butter in a 3-quart pot and bring to a boil over high heat. When butter has melted, reduce heat to medium and stir in flour. Keep stirring until dough pulls away from the sides of the pot. Remove from heat. Place dough on a flat dish to cool for 10 minutes.
2. Place cooled dough in a large bowl and beat on low mixer speed 3 minutes. Add eggs one at a time, beating well after each addition. Mixture should be stiff.
3. Using a pastry bag and plain or decorative tip, or a scoop, drop ¼ cup of dough 2 inches apart onto prepared cookie sheet. Bake until puffs are crisp and dry, about 60 minutes. Cool on a rack.
4. Make a hole in the side of each puff. Place filling in a pastry bag and pipe into the puff. Sprinkle with powdered sugar and serve immediately, or refrigerate up to 3 hours.

Variation

Cream Puff Swans: Using a pastry tube, make 3-inch S's with *pâte à choux* to use as swans' necks. Bake until lightly browned. Place a neck upright into the side of each puff to resemble a swan. Sprinkle with powdered sugar. Refrigerate until ready to serve.

Vanilla Cream Filling for Cream Puffs
Makes 2 cups

1 cup whole milk
½ cup sugar
3 tablespoons flour, or 1 tablespoon
   cornstarch

Pinch salt
2 large egg yolks or 1 large egg,
   lightly beaten
1 teaspoon vanilla extract

1. Place milk, sugar, flour, and salt in a 3-quart pot. Mix well and cook, stirring constantly, over low heat until mixture thickens.
2. Stir in egg yolks and bring to a boil. Cook on low, stirring constantly, 3 minutes. Stir in vanilla. Chill thoroughly before filling cream puffs.

Variations

Banana Cream Filling: Follow recipe for Vanilla Cream Filling. Add 1 cup mashed bananas and 2 tablespoons lemon juice after stirring in vanilla.
Coffee Cream Filling: Follow recipe for Vanilla Cream Filling. Add 2 teaspoons instant coffee after stirring in vanilla.
Chocolate Cream Filling: Follow recipe for Vanilla Cream Filling but increase sugar to 1 cup and scald milk with 2 ounces unsweetened chocolate before adding sugar and flour.

Pain au Chocolat
(Chocolate Sandwiches)

My grandmother sometimes made chocolate sandwiches for her children's noon meal. Can you imagine a lunch of bread, butter, sugar, and chocolate? My godchild Naina says that her friends loved to have overnights at her house because her mom made chocolate fudge sandwiches for breakfast. I suppose our chocolate sandwiches are the American equivalent of *pain au chocolat*, the chocolate-stuffed croissant that French children have for an afternoon snack.

Pain au Chocolat 1

Beat together ½ cup sugar, 1 stick soft butter, and 2 tablespoons cocoa. Use for a sandwich filling.

Pain au Chocolat 2

Place 2 cups sugar, ½ cup evaporated milk, 6 tablespoons butter, and 3 tablespoons cocoa in a heavy-bottomed saucepan. Stir and cook on medium-high heat to 250°F. Use as a filling for sandwiches.

Pain au Chocolat 3

Make a sandwich with 4 inches of French bread filled with a chocolate bar with or without nuts.

Éclairs au Chocolat (Chocolate Éclairs)

Makes 12 (4-inch) éclair shells

When our city relatives called on Sunday mornings to say they were coming to the country to visit, Mam Papaul would always hustle up a chocolate dessert. This one was a favorite of her daughter-in-law Audrey. She was married to my uncle Edgar, who, as a child, won the state 4-H pig-raising competition.

Éclairs are simply another shape for cream puff pastry, and we like ours filled with chocolate cream and frosted with a chocolate glaze. To make éclairs, use a large pastry tube to drop 3-inch oblongs of *pâte à choux* (same recipe used for cream puffs on page 186) onto a parchment-lined cookie sheet or jellyroll pan. Bake at 375°F until brown and crisp, approximately 1 hour. Split and fill with Vanilla Cream Filling for Cream Puffs (page 187) or the following chocolate custard recipe and top with chocolate frosting.

Chocolate Custard for Éclairs

Makes 2 cups

2 cups whole milk
1½ cups sugar
½ cup cornstarch
2 (1-ounce) squares chocolate
¼ teaspoon salt

1 large egg or two egg yolks, lightly beaten
1 teaspoon vanilla extract
2 teaspoons instant-coffee granules

1. Place milk, sugar, cornstarch, chocolate, and salt in a 3-quart pot. Mix well and cook over low heat, stirring occasionally, until chocolate is melted and mixture thickens.
2. Whisk in egg and bring to a bare simmer. Cook on low, stirring constantly, 3 minutes. Stir in vanilla and instant coffee. Cool completely before filling éclairs.

Chocolate Frosting

1 pound powdered sugar
5 tablespoons milk
⅓ cup cocoa

1 teaspoon vanilla extract
2 tablespoons butter or margarine
Pinch salt

Place all ingredients in a bowl and beat until smooth. Spread onto the tops of éclairs.

Mémère's Morning Crêpes

Makes 10 crêpes

Sometimes we had dessert for breakfast. We always rolled these tender flannel cakes up and dipped them in syrup. Mom could never make enough to fill us before school. On cold mornings, Mémère came across the yard to help Mom make crêpes. She and I would sing her favorite French song, "J'ai passé devant ta port" (I Passed in Front of Your Door), and we waltzed in the kitchen while the crêpes cooked. She would flip the crêpes and catch them as they came down with no problem. I could flip them, but they did not always land back in the skillet. Our singing and dancing was always cut short; crêpes cook quickly.

2 cups milk
2 large eggs
2 tablespoons butter, melted, plus ½ teaspoon

1½ cups sifted all-purpose flour
2 tablespoons sugar
1 teaspoon baking powder
½ teaspoon salt

1. In a medium bowl, beat together milk, eggs, and 2 tablespoons butter. In a separate bowl, sift together flour, sugar, baking powder, and salt. Add to milk mixture and beat well. (Sometimes I just put everything in a blender and do a quick mix.)
2. Add ½ teaspoon butter to an 8-inch nonstick crêpe pan or skillet set over medium heat. When butter is melted and hot, add ¼ cup batter to center of pan. Spread rapidly by tilting skillet in all directions. Cook 1 minute. Flip and lightly brown the other side, about 30 seconds more. Remove to a towel. Repeat procedure with remaining batter.

I have my mom's crêpe skillet.
A Latina friend once commented when she
saw the skillet hanging in my kitchen,
"Oh, you have a tortilla grill!"

Mémère's Oeufs à la Neige
(Floating Island)
Makes 12 servings

This classic French dessert is made of "islands" of meringue floating on a *crème anglaise* "sea," and we only made it during the Christmas season. The recipe is probably a carryover from the French who settled in the area. It can rightly be called German Coast eggnog, since everyone in the area serves it in place of eggnog and calls it eggnog. Children called this eggnog "snow on the mountain" and were allowed to add nutmeg to it, while the adults spiked theirs with a little whiskey. We enjoyed this hot after midnight mass and cold in the morning for a quick breakfast treat.

6 large eggs, separated
1½ cups sugar, divided
3 teaspoons vanilla extract, divided
1½ teaspoons almond extract,
    divided

2 quarts whole milk
½ cup cornstarch
1 (12-ounce) can evaporated milk

1. Beat egg whites with ½ cup sugar until very stiff, to form meringue. Mix in ½ teaspoon vanilla and ½ teaspoon almond extract. Set aside.
2. Bring milk to a boil in the top of a double boiler. Meanwhile, in a bowl, use medium mixer speed to beat together egg yolks and remaining 1 cup sugar until very light and lemon colored, about 4 minutes. Add remaining 2½ teaspoons vanilla and remaining 1 teaspoon almond extract. Whisk egg mixture into hot milk.
3. In a small bowl, add cornstarch to evaporated milk, then add to hot milk mixture and continue cooking on low heat, stirring often, until a light custard consistency, about 6 minutes.
4. Spoon tablespoonsful of meringue into hot custard, and spoon hot custard over meringue "islands." Cook until meringues are firm, about 30 seconds each side. Remove and set aside to cool. Continue spooning meringue into custard and cooking until all meringue is used.
5. Pour custard and meringues into a punch bowl to serve hot, or refrigerate after cooling.

Authentic Eggnog

Makes 12 servings

This holiday drink is best prepared and allowed to age in the refrigerator a week before serving. Do not serve to minors!

12 large eggs, separated
1½ cups sugar, divided
1 quart whipping cream
1 quart whole milk

3 cups brandy
¾ cup rum
Freshly grated nutmeg or mace for
   serving

1. Beat egg whites with ½ cup sugar until stiff. Set aside.
2. Beat egg yolks with remaining 1 cup sugar until light and frothy, about 4 minutes at medium mixer speed. In a large bowl, blend together the two egg mixtures. Gently whisk in remaining ingredients. Cover and refrigerate until ready to serve. Stir and serve in punch cups, and sprinkle with nutmeg or mace.

Creole Cream Cheese

Makes 1 pound

The first part of this process yields clabber, which is awfully close to the yogurt you'll find in a grocery store. Creole cream cheese is the result of strained clabber. Sprinkled with sugar and cream, Creole cream cheese became a classic dessert in New Orleans. Flavored with herbs, this soft cheese makes a wonderful spread.

3 gallons whole pasteurized milk   1 quart buttermilk

1. Place milks in a nonreactive bowl. Cover with a lid or cloth and set out at room temperature. Let sit in a warm place for several hours or overnight.
2. Separate the whey from the clabber by pouring the mixture into a strainer or colander lined with 2 layers of cheesecloth. Twist cloth tightly to remove excess moisture and place the resulting cheese in a bowl in the refrigerator until ready to use. For a dryer cream cheese, suspend drained cheese in cheesecloth over a bowl in the refrigerator overnight. Remove cheese from cloth and refrigerate. Keeps up to 2 weeks. Serve with cream and/or fruit.

Baked Custard 1

Makes 4 servings

This is the easiest flan you will ever make. No burnt sugar syrup here, because there are so many other toppings that can be used, including fruit in syrup and liqueurs.

1 (14-ounce) can sweetened
   condensed milk
1¼ cups whole or skim milk

2 large eggs, beaten
1 teaspoon vanilla extract
Topping of your choice

1. Preheat oven to 350°F. In a large bowl, mix condensed milk with whole milk. Beat eggs and vanilla into milk mixture.
2. Strain into a 1-quart buttered casserole dish or 6 ovenproof custard cups. Place dish or cups into a deeper pan filled with warm water that reaches halfway up the sides of the custard container(s).
3. Bake until a knife inserted into center of custard comes out clean, approximately 45 minutes. Cool at room temperature and chill before serving. Loosen custard with a thin knife blade and turn custard onto serving dish. Spread on a topping.

Baked Custard 2

Makes 6 servings

If you don't have condensed milk in the house, try this recipe.

3 large eggs, lightly beaten
⅓ cup sugar
1 teaspoon vanilla extract

Dash salt
2½ cups milk, scalded and cooled

1. Preheat oven to 350°F. In a large bowl, mix together eggs, sugar, vanilla, and salt. Stir in cooled milk.
2. Strain into a 1-quart buttered casserole dish or 6 ovenproof custard cups. Place dish or cups into a deeper pan filled with warm water that reaches halfway up the sides of the custard container(s).
3. Bake until a knife inserted into center of custard comes out clean, approximately 45 minutes. Cool at room temperature and chill before serving. Loosen custard with a thin knife blade and turn custard onto serving dish. Spread on a topping of your choice.

Mama's Rice Custard

Makes 8 servings

When the chickens were laying and we had more than enough milk from the cow, we could count on Mama making a great big bowl of rice custard. The secret to good texture is that the rice and milk should be cooked on very low heat for the rice to fully expand.

1 cup raw rice
2 quarts whole milk
4 large eggs
¾ cup sugar

1 teaspoon vanilla extract
2 tablespoons butter (optional)
Pinch salt

1. In a large, heavy-bottomed saucepan, cook rice with milk over low heat, covered, until rice is tender, about 25 minutes.
2. In a bowl, beat together eggs and sugar. Add to rice mixture, stirring constantly over low heat for 5 minutes.
3. Remove from heat and stir in vanilla, butter, and salt. Cool at room temperature and refrigerate until cold. Serve cold.

Persimmon Orange Dessert

Makes 4 servings

It's not often that I have persimmons to make this dessert because I love to eat them ripe from the tree and usually eat them all that way. My persimmon tree never produces more than about eighteen fruit, and I share those with a few neighbors who watch the tree all year and anticipate my sharing them. Some neighbors can tell me how many are on my tree before I have a chance to count. Then there's the problem of the raccoons and possums who call my yard home, and who often help themselves to my persimmons before I can pick them.

1 (3.4-ounce) box orange-flavored
   powdered gelatin

1½ cups hot water
1 cup persimmon pulp

Dissolve gelatin in hot water. Stir in persimmon pulp and chill until firm. Serve cold.

La Cuite Taffy
(pronounced la-queet)
Makes 12 pieces

Mom was one of nine children born to Octavie and Leopold Faucheux. That large brood passed their time away playing in the backyard barn, climbing trees, playing jacks using peach stones, and jumping rope. Mémère sometimes kept them busy by enlisting their help in making taffy.

La cuite is a thick sugarcane syrup, the last drawn before the syrup turns to sugar. It is made without lime, sulfur, or any other chemicals. Teaspoons of *la cuite* dipped in chopped pecans made for tasty lollipops. It was also used for topping ice cream and breads and for making this taffy.

1 cup *la cuite,* or 1 cup cane syrup
6 tablespoons sugar
3 tablespoons water

1 tablespoon butter
2 teaspoons vinegar
¼ teaspoon baking soda

1. Place syrup, sugar, water, butter, and vinegar in a 3-quart, heavy-bottomed pot. Cook over medium heat to hard ball stage (236°F).
2. Stir in baking soda. Spoon onto a buttered marble slab or platter to cool. When the mass can be easily handled, pick it up and start pulling and stretching it.
3. Pull until the taffy becomes very light tan in color. (Children with clean hands can be recruited to join in the fun.) Twist and cut the candy into 2-inch lengths.

Classic Divinity

Makes 24 pieces

One of the keys to making divinity is to be sure that the bowl and beater used to beat the egg whites is totally grease-free. I first made raspberry divinity with raspberry puree left over from making a sauce for my daughter Charlena's wedding cake. My son-in-law tells me that every cake I make is his favorite dessert, but he also loves this fudge.

2 cups sugar	3 large egg whites
½ cup water	½ teaspoon vanilla or almond extract
¼ cup light corn syrup	

1. Combine sugar, water, and corn syrup in a heavy-bottomed, 2-quart pot. Stir well. Bring mixture to a boil and cook briskly until syrup reaches 240°F on a candy thermometer, 10–15 minutes.
2. Meanwhile, using an electric mixer at medium speed, beat egg whites until they are stiff enough to stand in unwavering peaks on the whisk when it is lifted from the bowl.
3. As soon as the sugar mixture reaches the proper temperature, remove pot from the heat. Leaving the mixer on medium speed, begin pouring the hot syrup into the beaten egg whites in a slow and steady stream.
4. Add vanilla and continue to beat until the candy is smooth and begins to lose its gloss and is thick enough to hold its shape almost solidly in a spoon, about 10 minutes. Use a teaspoon to drop candies onto buttered parchment paper.

Variations

Berry Divinity: Add ¼ cup strawberry or raspberry puree or jam to the sugar, water, and corn syrup mixture before cooking.

Pecan Divinity: Add ½ cup chopped pecans to candy before beating and dropping onto buttered surface.

Mémère's Pralines

Makes 18 pieces

With two large pecan trees in the backyard, we always had pecans for fudge, pralines, and cookies. Mémère often came across the yard to visit and deliver a few pralines to her grandchildren. My daughter Nanette is a good cook, and she loves to make pralines using Mémère's recipe. Nanette has no culinary training but can duplicate anything.

1¼ cups evaporated milk
1 cup granulated sugar
4 tablespoons dark corn syrup

3 cups pecan halves or pieces
1½ teaspoons vanilla extract

1. Butter 2 feet of aluminum foil. Combine milk, sugar, and corn syrup in a heavy-bottomed, 3-quart pot. Cook on low heat, stirring constantly, until mixture reaches 228°F.
2. Stir in pecans and vanilla and cook to 236°F. Remove from heat and stir 3 minutes. Scoop and drop by tablespoonful onto prepared foil. Cool completely. Store in an airtight container.

Angela's Microwave Pralines

Makes 18 pralines

My mémère Nellie taught me how to make pecan candies. Even though everyone in my household was born with a sweet tooth, homemade candies were usually reserved for holidays. This is my daughter Angela's favorite recipe for pralines.

1 (1-pound) box dark-brown sugar
1 cup evaporated milk
¼ cup (½ stick) butter

2 cups shelled pecans
1 tablespoon vanilla extract

1. Butter 2 feet of aluminum foil. Stir together sugar and evaporated milk in a microwave-safe bowl. Cook in a 1,250-watt microwave oven for 7 minutes on high.
2. Stir in butter. Add pecans and vanilla. Continue stirring until syrup begins to thicken, 3 to 5 minutes. Drop by spoonfuls onto prepared foil. Let set approximately 30 minutes. Store in an airtight container.

Coconut Pralines

Makes 12 pralines

Aunt Aurelie made these for Pépère Tregre because he did not like to wear his false teeth, but he loved pralines.

2 cups white sugar
4 tablespoons water

1½ cups grated coconut

1. Butter 2 feet of aluminum foil. Cook sugar and water in a medium, heavy-bottomed saucepan over low heat to the soft ball stage, 228°F.
2. Add coconut and cook to hard ball stage, 236°F. Remove from heat and beat until creamy. Scoop and drop by tablespoonful onto prepared foil. Allow to cool. Store in an airtight container.

Pecan Gralee (pronounced grah-lay)

Makes 6 cups

Once you start eating *gralee*, it is hard to stop. Pecan *gralee* is a favorite treat on the German Coast and is sold commercially at mom-and-pop stores all over. It's an easy candy made from pecans and sugar. The origin of *gralee* remains a mystery. It wouldn't surprise me at all if it was created by an amateur cook in a sugar plantation kitchen, for the *gralee* is the result of cooking sugarcane to a syrup until it begins to crystallize.

2 cups white sugar
⅔ cup evaporated milk
2 tablespoons dark corn syrup
Pinch salt

3 tablespoons butter
½ teaspoon vanilla extract
4 cups shelled pecan halves

1. In a large, heavy-bottomed saucepan set over medium-high heat, cook sugar, milk, corn syrup, and salt to 250°F.
2. Add butter and vanilla. Stir in pecans. Continue cooking until pecans have developed a slightly roasted flavor.
3. Remove from heat and stir until pecans are coated with sugar mixture. Spread in a single layer on waxed paper to cool. Store in an airtight container.

Miss Mi–Mil's Mexican Fudge

Makes 24 pieces

Miss Mi-Mil was a cousin and a neighbor. Every Christmas, she brought over a box of her wonderful fudge. Although she included several kinds, my daughter Charlena and I vied for the Mexican fudge, a burnt-sugar fudge flavored with vanilla and studded with homegrown pecans.

4 cups sugar, divided
1 (12-ounce) can evaporated milk
1 cup (2 sticks) butter or margarine
Pinch salt

1½ cups chopped pecans
⅓ cup finely diced candied citron (optional)
1 teaspoon vanilla extract

1. Butter a 9×13-inch baking pan. Place 1 cup sugar in a heavy, 3-quart pot. Cook over medium heat, stirring constantly, until sugar is the color of a copper penny.
2. Slowly stir in milk. Add butter, remaining 3 cups sugar, and salt. (Mixture will lump, and you will think you have messed up.) Continue cooking until you have a smooth syrup. Without stirring, cook to soft boil stage (235–240°F). Remove from heat.
3. Let stand 5 minutes. Stir in pecans, citron, and vanilla. Beat with a large spoon until mixture thickens and loses its gloss. Pour into prepared pan. Let cool completely before cutting into squares.

*I insist that my grandchildren call me "Mémère"
because, aside from cooking French food, it is my way
of preserving a little piece of my French heritage.*

Chocolate Chip Fudge

Makes 24 (1-inch) pieces

Made with milk chocolate, this fudge is also known as gold brick fudge. It is equally good made with semisweet chocolate. This is so rich a treat that we only make it at Christmastime.

4½ cups sugar
1 (12-ounce) can evaporated milk
½ cup (1 stick) margarine or butter
12 ounces chocolate chips

1 pint marshmallow cream
1½ cups shelled pecans
1 teaspoon vanilla extract

1. Butter an 8×13-inch pan. In a large, heavy-bottomed saucepan, mix together sugar, milk, and margarine. Bring to a rolling boil over medium-high heat and cook 6 minutes, stirring constantly. Remove from heat.
2. Add chocolate chips and marshmallow cream. Stir until smooth.
3. Stir in pecans and vanilla and pour into prepared pan. Let cool completely before cutting into small squares.

Mam Papaul's Sugared Popcorn

Makes 3 quarts

What a treat this was when my grandmother had her seven grandchildren visiting on a cold winter's night. We told stories, ate popcorn, and slept in one big, unheated room in three double beds under warm, handmade quilts.

2 cups sugar
½ cup water

½ teaspoon almond extract (optional)
3 quarts popped corn

1. In a heavy-bottomed saucepan, cook sugar and water to the hard crack stage, 300°F (when a few drops of syrup are dropped into a cup of water, the sugar will be hard and brittle). Stir in almond extract.
2. Pour hot syrup over popcorn and stir to coat all pieces. Dump onto a tray and let dry. Store in an airtight container.

Popcorn Balls

Makes 6 balls

My dad, who was one of nine children, said that supper was sometimes just fresh syrup, homemade bread, and boiled milk. During sugar-grinding season, there was always an abundance of syrup for cornbread and biscuits.

Cutting sugarcane was backbreaking work, and it was the livelihood for many in the River Parishes before the industry was mechanized. A broad-bladed knife was specially designed to cut through the thick, fibrous cane stems that held the tall plant's sweet juices. Men took pride in keeping their knives clean and sharp. Years ago, an uncle who worked in the cane fields brought raw sugar to my mom, who said it was the best sugar for making pineapple upside-down cake. Today I have a friend whose husband still raises sugarcane, and she does the same for me. Mam Papaul made popcorn with cane syrup. The old people called this *tac tac*.

½ cup cane syrup (I use Steen's brand.)
½ cup water
1 teaspoon vinegar
Pinch salt
1 tablespoon butter
½ teaspoon baking soda
6 cups popped corn

1. Place syrup, water, vinegar, and salt in a heavy, 2-quart pot. Stir well to dissolve salt. Cook on medium heat to 270°F. Remove from heat. Stir in butter and baking soda.
2. Place popcorn in a large bowl. Pour syrup over popcorn. Butter your hands and shape 1 cup of popcorn into a ball. Repeat until you have made 6 balls. Cool and wrap in waxed paper.

Caramel Corn

Makes 6 cups

Toss 6 cups popped popcorn with the syrup from the Popcorn Balls recipe above, spread on a buttered cookie sheet, and bake at 225°F until syrup is dry on the popped corn, about 30 minutes. Cool popcorn before serving. Popcorn will harden and dry as it cools. Store in an airtight container.

Chocolate Popcorn

Makes 2 quarts

This is my favorite way to combine chocolate and popcorn. One of my daughters told me that she did not know until high school, when she started going to movies, that popcorn did not come with chocolate in it. When I bought popcorn for them, I would buy M&M's and drop a handful in each box. This recipe is adapted from a Jolly Time Popcorn handout.

2 tablespoons butter
6 ounces semisweet chocolate pieces
½ cup raisins
1 teaspoon instant coffee
1 teaspoon vanilla extract

12 regular-sized marshmallows
1 tablespoon water
2 quarts popped popcorn
Salt for seasoning (optional)

1. Melt butter in large, heavy saucepan over low heat or in a microwave oven.
2. Add remaining ingredients except popcorn. Stir until chocolate and marshmallows have melted. Add popcorn and mix until popcorn is well coated. Sprinkle with salt if you like.

Baked Caramel Corn

Makes 6 quarts

This is one of my husband's favorite snacks. He cannot walk into a movie theater without buying caramel corn or popcorn. This is another recipe based on my old Jolly Time handout.

1 cup butter
½ cup brown sugar
½ cup white sugar
½ cup dark corn syrup
1 teaspoon salt

½ teaspoon cinnamon
1 teaspoon vanilla extract
½ teaspoon baking soda
6 quarts popped popcorn

1. Preheat oven to 250°F. Melt butter in a large, heavy saucepan set over low heat. Add sugars, corn syrup, salt, and cinnamon. Bring to a boil and cook 5 minutes, stirring constantly.

2. Remove from heat. Add vanilla and baking soda. Pour over popcorn and mix well to coat.
3. Spread popcorn on rimmed baking sheet. Bake 1 hour, stirring every 15 minutes. Break popcorn apart and store in airtight container.

Chocolate Cream Cheese Ball

Makes 1 cheese ball, serving 16

I developed this cheese ball for my husband's Christmas parties when he was sheriff of St. Charles Parish.

1 pound store-bought cream cheese	**2 tablespoons evaporated milk**
½ cup sugar	**1 cup toasted and chopped pecans**
3 tablespoons cocoa	**3 dozen ginger snaps for serving**

1. Cream together cream cheese, sugar, cocoa, and evaporated milk.
2. Line a small bowl with plastic wrap. Scrape cream cheese mixture into bowl and wrap tightly with plastic. Refrigerate at least 1 hour.
3. Turn out on a serving dish and remove wrap. Press pecans onto the ball. Serve with ginger snaps.

My husband, Charles, and me

An overabundance of milk from Sally, our backyard cow, meant that we would enjoy a variety of milk-based treats, and one of our favorites was ice cream. Today's ice cream makers make the job of producing delicious ice cream at home relatively easy. The old-fashioned crank ice cream maker that requires salt and ice to keep the temperature low now runs on electricity. I use an even more modern electric ice cream maker, which has an easy-to-use canister that I freeze ahead of time. To "ripen" ice cream made in an electric crank freezer, unplug the unit, pack the canister with additional salt and ice, and cover with a heavy cloth or blanket for a few hours. Ice cream made in the frozen canister-type machine doesn't get too hard, so after it's ready, it's best to scoop it into a storage container and harden in the freezer.

When making ice cream, follow the instructions of the ice cream maker's manufacturer, and use these hints as a guide:

- For a crank machine, use 1½ cups table salt or 1 cup rock salt per 5–6 pounds crushed ice.
- To lower the temperature, increase the salt.
- Increase salt if ice cream liquid has a high sugar content.
- Fill the canister only halfway to avoid the liquid overflowing into the brine.
- Richness can be controlled by the type of milk you use. Whipping cream or a creamy milk combination give the smoothest mouth feel.
- Any juice and sugar combination, even wine, can be frozen in an ice cream maker for a light and refreshing sorbet.

Grandfather Papaul (Leopold Faucheux) feeding his cow at the backyard barn door.

Very Vanilla Ice Cream

Makes 1½ quarts

4 cups whole milk
1½ cups half-and-half or whipping
   cream
1 (14-ounce) can sweetened
   condensed milk, or ¾ cup sugar

¼ teaspoon salt
3 tablespoons cornstarch
3 tablespoons water
3 large egg yolks
1 tablespoon vanilla extract

1. In a 5-quart saucepan or the top of a double boiler, add milk, half-and-half, condensed milk, and salt. Turn heat to low and stir constantly until mixture begins to bubble.
2. Mix cornstarch with water until smooth and stir into milk mixture. Leave on low heat while you place egg yolks and vanilla in a small bowl and whisk 1 minute. Whisk ½ cup hot milk mixture into egg yolk mixture, then whisk egg yolk mixture into hot milk mixture in the pot.
3. Cook on low, stirring often, until mixture lightly coats the back of a spoon, around 170°F. Strain mixture into a bowl. Place in the refrigerator to cool for at least 45 minutes. Freeze per directions of ice cream maker's manufacturer.

Fresh Strawberry Ice Cream

Makes 1½ quarts

3 cups fresh strawberries, hulls
   removed
½ cup sugar

2 (12-ounce) cans evaporated milk,
   or 3 cups half-and-half
½ teaspoon vanilla extract

Puree berries with sugar until smooth. Stir in milk and vanilla. Freeze per directions of ice cream maker's manufacturer. Serve or freeze to ripen, then serve.

Creole Cream Cheese Ice Cream

Makes 8–10 servings

3 cups Creole Cream Cheese
   (recipe on page 192)
2 cups whipping cream
1 (14-ounce) can sweetened
   condensed milk

1 teaspoon vanilla extract
3 large egg whites (optional)

1. Press Creole cream cheese through a fine sieve. Use medium mixer speed to beat the cream cheese and whipping cream together until creamy and smooth, about 3 minutes. Beat in condensed milk, vanilla, and egg whites for 2 minutes.
2. Pour mixture into a 2-quart electric ice cream freezer and process per manufacturer's directions.

Cinnamon Ice Cream

Makes 8 servings

We reserved ice cream making for Sundays and church fairs. Everyone had a special talent to share at the fair, and Mam Papaul's was making ice cream. She used an old-fashioned wooden ice cream maker that had to be cranked by hand. Young men wanting to impress the girls with their brawn often volunteered for the job.

1 quart whole milk
1 cup sugar
6 large egg yolks

1 quart half-and-half
2 tablespoons cinnamon

1. In a medium saucepan, cook milk and sugar together over medium heat until sugar is dissolved. Turn heat down to low and whisk in egg yolks. Cook on low heat, whisking constantly, for 2 minutes. Blend in the half-and-half and cinnamon.
2. Cool completely. Freeze in an ice cream maker per manufacturer's directions.

Baked Alaska

Makes 8 servings

When my mom discovered this dessert, she intrigued us by saying she was going to bake ice cream. I don't know where she got the recipe, but she first made it for a Sunday dessert. Here is a shortcut version of her baked Alaska.

2 (8-inch) round cake layers, any flavor
½ gallon ice cream, any flavor, slightly softened

4 large egg whites
Pinch cream of tartar
½ teaspoon vanilla or almond extract
½ cup sugar

1. Place 1 cake layer on a thick board, such as a scrupulously clean or new chopping board. Cover with foil and set aside.
2. Line the insides of an 8-inch round cake pan with aluminum foil or plastic wrap, allowing the foil to hang over the sides at least an inch. Cut ice cream into slabs and place into prepared pan. Level ice cream using a metal spatula. Cover and freeze hard.
3. When ice cream is hard, preheat oven to 400°F. Grasp the foil to lift the ice cream from the pan and place it on the cake on the board. Top with second cake layer. (Fresh or canned fruit or fruit pie filling may be spread over ice cream before adding second layer.)
4. To make meringue, beat egg whites and cream of tartar until light and stiff. Add vanilla. Beat in sugar a little at a time. (For a meringue with more body, cook sugar with ¼ cup water to a soft boil stage [270°F], then add to the beaten egg whites.) Spread meringue over cake, making sure edges are sealed. Bake on chopping board until meringue is lightly browned, 5–8 minutes. Serve immediately.

Candied "Grapefruit" (Pomelo/Shaddock) à la Corinne Dunbar

Makes 3 pints

Corinne Dunbar, in her famous restaurant on New Orleans's St. Charles Avenue, used to end each meal with a piece of preserved grapefruit. No one was ever able to duplicate this sweet. This is just my opinion, but I think the preserved "grapefruit" was actually preserved pomelo, a large citrus fruit my mom used to make preserves. Locally, we call the fruit "shaddock." Pomelo looks like a giant grapefruit, but it's a different species. Once every couple of years, my dad would bring home a large bag of shaddock. The juice was bitter so we'd throw it away, but my mom turned the thick pith, the white stuff under the rind, into a preserve.

I don't know anyone who had or has a shaddock tree, but obviously my dad did, and he enjoyed his preserved shaddock after supper with crackers. Imagine my surprise when I recently found this fruit in the Hong Kong Grocery Store in Gretna, Louisiana. Now I can duplicate my mom's shaddock preserves.

1 large pomelo
3 cups sugar
1½ cups water

3 drops yellow food coloring (optional)
3 sterilized pint canning jars, lids, and screw tops

1. Peel yellow skin from shaddock (pomelo), leaving pulp in place. Score pith with a sharp knife every half inch. Pull pith apart from pulp in ½ inch sections. Discard pulp or use in place of lemon in lemonade.
2. Place pith in a bowl and add enough cold water to cover completely. Let stand 12 hours. Change water every day for 3 days.
3. On fourth day, place pith in a saucepan and cover with fresh cold water. Bring water to a boil and simmer 5 minutes. Drain. Add sugar, 1½ cups water, and food coloring to saucepan. Bring to a boil and simmer until clear, thick, and very syrupy.
4. Place hot mixture in sterile jars, leaving ½ inch air space. Be sure fruit is covered with hot liquid. Wipe opening of jar with a damp, sterile cloth. Cover and seal. Store in refrigerator or process in a water bath. To process, place jars on a rack in a large pot and cover tops by two inches of hot water. Bring water to a boil. Lower heat, cover, and simmer 15 minutes. Remove from water. Cool and test for seal. Store at room temperature.

Fig Preserves
Makes 5 pints

We had thirteen fig trees in our backyard. We ate fresh figs during the summer and preserves the rest of the year.

8 cups figs
2 teaspoons baking soda
4 cups sugar

1 cup water
4 sterilized pint canning jars with
    new lids and screw tops

1. Place figs in a clean sink and add baking soda. Cover figs with water. Drain water and rinse figs with cool tap water.
2. Place figs, sugar, and 1 cup water in a heavy 5-quart saucepan. Stir well and bring to a boil. Cook on low heat until figs turn deep brown and sugar turns brown and syrupy, about 45 minutes.
3. Place hot mixture in sterile jars, leaving ½ inch air space. Be sure fruit is covered with hot liquid. Wipe opening of jar with a damp, sterile cloth. Cover and seal. Store in refrigerator or process in a water bath. To process, place jars on a rack in a large pot and cover tops by two inches of hot water. Bring water to a boil. Lower heat, cover, and simmer 15 minutes. Remove from water. Cool and test for seal. Store at room temperature.

Note: My friend Gina Hymel cooks 2½ gallons of figs with 3 cups of water and 5 pounds of sugar.

Kumquat Preserves

Makes 8 pints

For the last few years, I have been the lucky recipient of fresh kumquats from our former assessor of St. Charles Parish. He gave kumquats to my uncle Gee Gee until the day my uncle died. My uncle always shared with me, but now I am the sole beneficiary of the assessor's kumquats.

6 cups kumquats, stemmed
1 teaspoon baking soda
3 cups sugar
½ cup water

¼ cup fresh lemon juice
8 sterilized pint canning jars, lids, and screw tops

1. Place kumquats in a clean sink and add baking soda. Cover kumquats with water and let soak 30 minutes. Drain and wash any residue from each kumquat using a rough cloth. Discard any that are broken or have brown spots. Cut an x in the ends of each kumquat.
2. Place kumquats in a large pot with sugar, ½ cup water, and lemon juice. Stir well. Bring to a boil, lower heat to a simmer, and cook on low heat until kumquats appear translucent and syrup is thick.
3. Place hot mixture in sterile jars, leaving ½ inch air space. Be sure fruit is covered with syrup. Wipe opening of jar with a damp, sterile cloth. Cover and seal. Store in refrigerator or process in a water bath. To process, place jars on a rack in a large pot and cover tops by two inches of hot water. Bring water to a boil. Lower heat, cover, and simmer 15 minutes. Remove from water. Cool and test for seal. Store at room temperature.

Mémère's Blackberry Jelly

Makes 2 pints

Mémère was always in charge of the kitchen during summer jelly-making sessions. Even though it seemed like we made enough to feed an army, there never seemed to be enough blackberry jelly to last the year. For that reason, it was rationed out and used for jellyrolls rather than placed on the breakfast table. Blackberry jelly was my favorite flavor. When I moved away from home, Mama always snuck a jar into my suitcase as a surprise.

3½ cups blackberry juice (juice from 3 quarts of berries)

3 cups sugar

2 sterilized pint canning jars with new lids and screw tops

1. Place berry juice and sugar in a large stainless steel pot. Cook gently until sugar has dissolved. Turn heat up to medium and bring to a rolling boil.
2. After 8 minutes of vigorous boiling, check to see if jelly is ready. It will sheet (coat) a metal spoon, or set when you drop a small amount on a chilled plate. When cooked enough, remove from heat and pour into sterilized jars, filling to ½ inch from top. Wipe opening of jar with a damp, sterile cloth. Cover and seal. Let cool, then place in refrigerator or store in pantry like my mom always did after she checked to see if the jars had a tight seal. There should be a slight dent in the lid if the jar has been sealed properly. If the lid pings when pressed, the jar does not have a good seal and must be processed in a water bath. See any of the preserve recipes above for processing instructions.

Pepper Jelly

Makes 3 pints

South Louisiana's summer gardens yield lots of varieties of peppers. The innovative ladies on the river developed this wonderful jelly that has many uses, including spreading over cream cheese as an appetizer. It also serves as an easy sauce for pork roast, chicken, and salmon. Although I've never tried it, I bet it would be good over vanilla ice cream. Why not? My daughter Angela won a national Tabasco contest with a recipe for coconut jalapeño ice cream.

1½ cups finely chopped red
  bell pepper
1½ cups finely chopped yellow
  bell pepper
1½ cups finely chopped green
  bell pepper
½ cup finely chopped jalapeño
  pepper

6½ cups sugar
1½ cups cider vinegar
1 (1.75-ounce) package dry pectin
½ teaspoon butter
6 sterile pint canning jars, lids,
  and screw tops

1. Combine peppers, sugar, and vinegar in a 3-quart pot. Bring to a boil. Remove from heat and let stand 5 minutes. Stir in pectin and bring to a boil. Add butter.
2. Stirring constantly, bring to a full boil that will not stir down. Pour into sterile jars, leaving a ½-inch headspace. Wipe jar opening with a damp, sterile cloth. Cover and seal.
3. To process, place jars on a rack in a large pot and cover tops by two inches of hot water. Bring water to a boil. Lower heat and simmer 10 minutes. Remove from water. Cool and test for seal. Store at room temperature.

BEVERAGES

MOST OF MY FAMILY did not drink alcohol, except for a glass of wine and a little anisette at Christmas. A few do enjoy beer with their boiled seafood, wine with supper or dinner, or a hot toddy on occasion. Once, my mama tried to make pineapple beer for my grandfather, but it smelled so bad she threw it out.

Mémère and my grandmother Mam Papaul were known up and down the river for their hospitality. Drop-in company was not unusual, and everyone was welcome at any time. The usual beverage offering was café au lait made in an old-fashioned drip pot, and no one made it better than those two ladies. Drinking coffee black was not the mode of the day in our area. I don't believe I knew anyone who drank coffee without sugar and boiled milk until I went to college in Lafayette.

Although she was a diabetic, sometimes Mam Papaul sweetened her coffee with condensed milk. But that's not the best condensed milk story. When my uncle Clancy was a child, he would steal a can of condensed milk from the pantry, hide under the house, make a hole in the lid with an ice pick, and suck the milk from the can. When Uncle Clancy retired as a lieutenant colonel from the army, he, too, was diabetic, but he still loved his condensed milk. All the while he was in the military, my grandmother sent him cans of condensed milk, along with her homemade canned chicken and andouille gumbo.

The water we used to brew coffee came from a cistern. Every house in our area had a cistern that provided water for everything from bathing to cooking. Ours was made from cypress slats and stood near the house underneath a gutter that caught rainwater. If there was little rain, we rationed out the water for bathing. As children, we sometimes shared a tub of water. The soft cistern water made a great conditioning rinse after a shampoo.

Café au Lait
(Coffee with Milk)

Makes 4 servings

Nary a child on the German Coast went off to school without first having a cup of café au lait with a breakfast of bacon or ham and eggs and grits. In place of café au lait, Mom did sometimes serve hot tea sweetened with condensed milk.

4 tablespoons ground dark-roasted
    coffee or coffee with chicory
4 cups hot water

2 cups whole milk
Sugar or condensed milk to taste

1. Prepare coffee with the hot water in a drip pot or your favorite coffee maker.
2. Bring milk to a boil and add immediately to the hot brewed coffee. Add sugar to taste.

*When I returned home from college on weekends,
I often enjoyed a cup of café au lait with Mam Papaul
at her home. My mother had told me Mam Papaul liked
condensed milk or sugar and boiled milk in her coffee, and
it wasn't until I was older that I actually witnessed her adding
her secret ingredient. That special touch made all the
difference in the world. Mam Papaul never used
mugs; she always used a cup and saucer.*

Old-Fashioned Louisiana Drip Coffee

Makes 1 serving

This is the coffee of the "old people," as we called my great-grandparents and grandparents. It was made by hand using a tediously slow drip process. The pot was usually enamel, and the coffee was either pure coffee or coffee with chicory. Either way, the process for making it was the same.

1½ to 2 tablespoons Louisiana drip   1 cup boiling water
    ground coffee or coffee with
    chicory

Place grounds in the top section of a French drip pot. Slowly pour ¼ cup boiling water at a time over the grounds every few minutes until all water has dripped through the grounds. Heat coffee by placing a saucepan of water over low heat and the coffeepot in the pan. Never boil the coffee.

Boiled Milk

Makes 2½ quarts

No matter what was served, we had milk with supper. In my childhood, we always had a highly productive cow in the backyard, so why not? Every day, Mom boiled milk from that cow, cooled it, and placed it in the refrigerator, where a thick layer of cream would form on the top. It was my goal to skim off that cream for a treat before my dad got to it. Dad loved his fresh cream with figs and crackers after supper, but he never complained when we children got to it first. When I got older and the cow was gone, we bought pasteurized milk from the milkman. The commercial milk was not homogenized, so we still boiled it and enjoyed the cream.

1 gallon fresh milk

1. Place milk in a 6–8-quart pot and bring to a boil. Lower heat and simmer 15 minutes.
2. Cool and refrigerate several hours before serving. A thick, rich cream will form on the top.

Granny's Iced Tea

Makes 2½ quarts

My children always called this beverage "Granny tea." It is like a good sweetened lemonade flavored with tea. We loved it, and my children talk about Granny tea with fond memories of helping their grandmother make it.

2 quarts water
2 large tea bags

1 cup sugar, or more
1 cup freshly squeezed lemon juice

1. Bring water to a boil in a saucepan. Remove pan from heat. Add tea bags, cover, and let steep 10 minutes. Remove tea bags.
2. Stir sugar into hot tea until dissolved. Stir in lemon juice and serve over ice.

Mint Lemonade

Makes 8 servings

Mom was a busy lady with five children, a cottage industry as a seamstress, and, later, a cake business. Even so, she sometimes took the time to add extra touches to her cooking. Bread crumbs that topped her vegetable casseroles were always buttered, and our lemonade was often flavored and garnished with mint that grew near the base of the cistern. If you have a Meyer lemon tree in the backyard, as so many of us do, juice the lemons and freeze the juice so you can make this tea any time of the year.

2 quarts water
1 cup sugar
1 cup freshly squeezed lemon juice

16 fresh crushed mint leaves, plus
additional for garnish

1. Bring water to a boil in a large saucepan and add sugar. Stir, reduce heat, and simmer until sugar dissolves. Remove pan from heat.
2. Add lemon juice and mint leaves. Let steep 10 minutes. Strain out the leaves.
3. Serve over ice and garnish with fresh mint leaves.

Homemade Root Beer

Makes 8 servings

My mom often made root beer during the summer. We were not allowed to have soft drinks with our meals, but homemade root beer was permitted at lunch. This recipe is a variation on the one on the Zatarain's-brand root beer concentrate bottle. My mom says that when she was a child, her mother made root beer, but she added yeast to get it to fizz. She stored the bottles in a cellar under the house. (The cellar was just a shelf that hung from the floor supports.) She said that many times she and her siblings heard the caps popping off the bottles during hot summers. Looking back, I think the yeast fermented, and they were making an alcoholic root beer. I wonder if the children ever got to drink that root beer.

1 quart warm water
½ cup granulated sugar

2 teaspoons Zatarain's root beer
  concentrate

In a pitcher, mix all ingredients and stir until sugar is dissolved. Refrigerate until ready to serve, or serve immediately over ice.

Orange Blossom Syrup

Makes 1 quart

I believe the origin of this special treat was my mémère Nellie Zeringue. I like this syrup in tea, but it is equally delicious as a topping for a snow cone.

3 cups water
2 cups sugar

3 cups orange blossoms, rinsed

1. Bring water and sugar to a boil in large saucepan set over medium-high heat. Add orange blossoms. Lower heat and simmer 10 minutes. Cover and set aside 20 minutes.
2. Pour syrup through a colander. Discard blossoms. Place syrup in a sterile jar and refrigerate. Add to iced tea, over snowballs, or over ice as a cordial.

Anisette

Makes about 1½ quarts

Daddy always brought home a bottle of red anisette during the holidays. Even the children were allowed a little taste of this homemade liqueur, mixed with lots of water and ice. This was a Christmas treat I especially enjoyed; I love that sweet licorice flavor.

3¾ cups granulated sugar
1½ cups distilled water, divided
1 quart vodka or 1 pint ethyl alcohol,
    such as Everclear, plus 1 pint
    water

½ teaspoon red food coloring
½ teaspoon anise oil*

In a large glass or nonreactive metal container, mix sugar and ¾ cup distilled water. Stir until sugar is dissolved. Add vodka, food coloring, anise oil, and remaining water. Cover and let stand two weeks at room temperature. Serve over crushed ice or plain as a liqueur.

*Found at most drug stores in the pharmacy section.

Crème de Menthe

Makes about 1½ quarts

Crème de menthe is a sweet, green, peppermint liqueur that my mama often used as a digestif. The beautiful color intrigued me, and I often begged for a taste.

Follow the recipe above for anisette, using ½ teaspoon oil of peppermint in place of anise oil and green food coloring in place of red coloring.

Wild Cherry Bounce

Makes about 2 quarts

Not only was this a delightful dessert wine, but it also served as a remedy for everything from diarrhea to celebrating holidays. Wild cherries are very small, and they do not have seeds. They grow wild on the German Coast.

1 quart wild cherries
1 pound sugar

1 quart white port or 1 cup ethyl
    alcohol, such as Everclear
1 cup water

1. Wash cherries and place in a crock or stainless steel container. Pour sugar over berries and cover lightly with a clean, sterile cloth. Let stand at room temperature until sugar is completely dissolved, about 8 weeks. Stir occasionally.
2. Use a sterile cheesecloth to strain into a clean container, squeezing gently. Stir in port and water. Chill and serve straight from the bottle or over ice.

Blackberry Punch

Makes 6 quarts

This is a flavorful alcohol-laced punch to serve at a party. It's not too strong, so everyone can enjoy it.

2 liters Sprite or 7-Up
2 cups blackberry wine
1 pint fresh blackberries

2 sliced oranges
Plenty of ice

Place ingredients in a punch bowl. Stir in ice. Serve and enjoy.

Mam Papaul's sister Chloe and Mémère

BIBLIOGRAPHY

Berolzheimer, Ruth, ed. *Culinary Arts Institute Encyclopedic Cookbook*. Chicago, IL: Culinary Arts Institute, 1948.

Blume, Helmet. *The German Coast during the Colonial Era, 1722–1803*. Destrehan, LA: German-Acadian Coast Historical and Genealogical Society, 1990.

Child, Julia. *The French Chef Cookbook*. New York: Knopf, 1968.

Creekmore, Judy. *Celebrating 200 Years of River Parish History*. New Orleans: Times Picayune Publishing, 1977.

Deiler, J. Hanno. *The Settlement of the German Coast of Louisiana and Creoles of German Descent*. Baltimore: Genealogical Publishing, 1969.

Folse, Chef John D. *The Encyclopedia of Cajun & Creole Cuisine*. Gonzales, LA: Chef John Folse & Co., 2004.

Gutierrez, C. Paige. *Cajun Foodways*. Jackson: University Press of Mississippi, 1992.

Kral, Kathy. *Czech Reflections, Recipes, Memories, and History*. West, TX: McLennan-Hill County Czech Heritage Society, 1994.

Mariani, John F. *The Dictionary of American Food and Drink*. New York: Hearst, 1994.

Martin, Addie K., and Jeremy Martin. *Southeast Louisiana Food: A Seasoned Tradition*. Charleston, S.C.: History Press, 2014.

Merrill, Ellen C. *Germans of Louisiana*. Gretna, LA: Pelican, 2005.

Montagné, Prosper. *Larousse Gastronomique: The Encyclopedia of Food, Wine, and Cookery*. New York: Crown, 1961.

Tucker, Susan, ed. *New Orleans Cuisine: Fourteen Signature Dishes and Their Histories*. Jackson: University Press of Mississippi, 2009.

Wilson, Nancy. *Mam Papaul's Country Creole Basket*. Hahnville, LA: Naked Lady Press, 2012.

Mémère and Mam Papaul were always ready to welcome unexpected guests with a cup of café au lait, the pot ever ready on the stove.

Index of Recipes

W

Wedding Cake, Silver, 160–61
Whipped-Cream Frosting, 149
White Beans with Ham, 111
White Boudin, 28
White Crab and Shrimp Bisque, 7
White Gravy, Panéed Meat with, 35
Whole Stuffed Chicken, 59

Wild Cherry Bounce, 219
Wine Cookies, 181

Y

Yeast-Raised Chocolate Cake with Orange
 Whipped-Cream Frosting, 148–49
Yellow Rice, 129